Location Theory

Location Theory

MARTIN BECKMANN

Brown University and the University of Bonn

RANDOM HOUSE

New York

To the Memory of Leonhard Miksch
(1901 – 1950)

In dedicating this book to Leonhard Miksch, who was Professor of Economics at the University of Freiburg, I should like to honor the memory of a man who, in his brief career, left a deep imprint on German economics, inspiring in his students an abiding interest in location theory.

Preface

The purpose of this book is to give a systematic exposition of the theory of location at the level of intermediate and advanced undergraduate economics. The emphasis is on theory. Technical points requiring mathematical arguments have been treated in footnotes, but the main text is self-contained. The advanced student may be stimulated to pursue some of the open problems that appear in these technical notes. Besides drawing on the vast literature that the field of location theory and related regional science has generated, I have received intense and lasting stimulation from work at the Cowles Commission under the direction of Professor Tjalling C. Koopmans. In Chapter 6, in the section on the pricing of heterogeneous goods in spatially separated markets, I have incorporated some results which he and I have obtained in joint work and which, in a different form, have been published.[1] Professor Koopmans has kindly allowed me to use these results. In the immediately preceding section of that chapter, in which I develop a linear programming formulation of spatial equilibrium, I have benefited from the early explorations that Thomas Marschak and I made in this area.[2]

[1]"Assignment Problems and the Location of Economic Activities," *Econometrica*, Vol. 25, No. 1 (1957), pp. 53–76.
[2]Martin Beckmann and Thomas Marschak, "An Activity Analysis Approach to Location Theory," *Proceedings of the Second Symposium in Linear Programming* (Washington, D. C.: National Bureau of Standards and Directorate of Management Analysis, 1955).

Professor Donald Dewey of Columbia University and Mr. John McPherson, graduate student at Brown University, read the first draft of this manuscript and contributed many helpful suggestions for which I should like to express my appreciation. Mr. Gilbert Suzawa assisted me in the preparation of the index. The scope of the Selected Readings which follow each chapter was expanded considerably through the researches of Mr. McPherson, one of the most avid readers I have ever known. I am also grateful to Mr. Jochen Mohnfeld, Miss Margaret Herbst, Miss Mona Hassanein-Norres, Dr. Dieter Hochstaedter, Mr. Lothar Weinert, and Mr. Götz Uebe for their help in preparing the manuscript. To all of these I should like to express my gratitude. Dr. Hochstaedter assisted me in the calculation of the entries in Table 3.1 and the drafting of the figures.

Bad Godesberg, Germany   MARTIN BECKMANN
December, 1966

Contents

Tables

Figures

Location Theory

CHAPTER **1**

Introduction

In location theory economic analysis is used to study the geography of man's economic activities. Location theory raises the question of "where" and adds it to those of "what," "for whom," "how," and "when," which the student of economic theory encounters in the discussion of the functions of an economic system. We may say that location theory is also the study of the effects of space on the organization of economic activities. Historically, it has developed from a study of the location of plants and of an industry to a more inclusive analysis of the spatial pattern of all economic activities.

Space enters into economic relationships in two ways:

1. Effects of economic activities on other activities carried out in adjacent locations: *neighborhood effects*
2. Costs incurred in moving factors (persons) or goods: *transportation costs*

Explicit consideration of these effects of space does not, of course, change the basic results of general economic theory; it lends them additional structure. Ordinary spaceless economics may be considered as dealing with a spatially homogeneous economy where all activities are carried out almost everywhere at about the same level. (A location would then be considered a small region rather than, say, a factory site.) This is what some people conceive of as the future megalopolis. Or, transportation costs may be regarded as negligible and thus assumed away.

Another possibility is to assume that transportation activities that are necessary in a nonhomogeneous region are part of production and are in fact included in the production function. Location theory seeks to split off these transportation activities, to expose the spatial aspects of production and of other economic activities, and to examine the emerging spatial structures as objects of interest in themselves. If light can be thrown back on the general principles of economics, so much the better, but there has been little feedback in the past. General economists have had more use for the analysis of time in economics, say, than for that of space. Fortunately, there are other customers: geographers, sociologists, regional scientists, city planners, etc.

Since equilibrium analysis is the basic tool of economic analysis and since neighborhood effects are a disturbance in the smooth mechanism of allocation through the market, relatively little attention is normally given to these, even though some important questions in general economic analysis are raised by just these neighborhood effects. These have usually been treated separately under the heading of welfare economics. In essence it is, however, this spillover that creates the necessity or desirability of city and regional planning.

On the other hand, the existence of transportation cost generates the need to economize space in order to keep distances tolerable. Thus, even in situations where free land exists, most activities are pulled together spatially, that is, there is geographical concentration.

Transportation costs create market patterns in the spatial distribution of prices as well as in the allocation of suppliers to demanders and in the allocation of land to competing products and in the tying together of several production activities in "central places." The need to economize transportation creates a particular logic of spatial relationships.

This logic is much more accessible to equilibrium analysis than are neighborhood effects. So emphasis is usually (and in this book too) placed on these facets of location.

While the introduction of spatial aspects tends to complicate economic analysis in some ways, occasionally it serves to remove certain difficulties. Thus, as will be shown, constant returns to scale in production are not inconsistent with an optimal scale of plant, and increasing returns to scale are not inconsistent with competitive equilibrium.

Consideration of space may also lead to a shift of emphasis: Competition may be perfect, as in a continuously extended spatial market, or may be near perfect, as when several firms are competing for sales territory in a central-place model; but in a spatial setting the prevailing mode is one of imperfect competition.

The various models that make up modern location theory have been invented at rather different stages in the development of economics. In retrospect, location theorists seem to have been groping for the tools that were made explicit in linear programming, or activity analysis. Linear activity analysis in conjunction with economic equilibrium theory is a very powerful tool and moreover appears to be the natural language in terms of which to describe economic relations in space, more particularly those that deal with allocation, efficiency, and equilibrium. Unfortunately, there has developed from this affinity a tendency to reduce location problems to a format where the geometry of space completely disappears and is replaced by an abstract framework of matrices. While I am certainly not opposed to mathematical methods in location theory (having been involved in this business myself), I would deplore the exclusive or even predominant use of this approach. To this day the geometric-intuitive approach that has characterized location theory in the past seems to me to be fruitful and capable of further development, and that is the approach we are going to take here.

What about the study of those economic relationships in space that operate through another important mechanism, that of income flows? These "macroeconomic" aspects of locations and regions—such as the locational multiplier, the regional balances of trade, the regional input-output tables—make up the heart of what is now called regional science.[1] By contrast, location theory proper is concerned with the microeconomics of space, with allocation and equilibrium as achieved by the price mechanism; and I should like to restrict myself to that. Whether this restriction is tenable remains of course to be seen.

This price-theoretic approach has dictated the structure of this book. First of all we must distinguish between a short-run and a long-run analysis. In the short run, plant locations and residential locations are fixed, and the spatial price system performs its function of rationing resources among users. These problems are treated under the heading of spatial equilibrium (Chapter 6, particularly the first section).

In space the analysis of equilibrium at the industry level turns rather crucially on whether the resources of that industry are limited to particular places (resource deposits, other industries) or whether they are found everywhere. Thus the problems involving a single product are different from those where several commodities compete for space and/or interact in their role as inputs and outputs. Therefore, wherever possible I have separated the one-commodity problems, which reveal some general spatial structures in greater simplicity, from the more complex multicommodity problems (Chapter 3).

It goes without saying that analysis at the industry level must be preceded by a study of location at the plant and activity level (Chapter 2).

A problem peculiar to location theory is the allocation of land and the structures in land use that are imposed by the economics of transportation. These are most explicitly seen in the location of agricultural activities (Chapter 4).

As in economic theory generally, general equilibrium analysis is relatively less advanced than the partial equilib-

[1] Isard W., *et al.*, *Methods of Regional Analysis* (New York: John Wiley, 1960).

rium models which make up the bulk of the economist's tool kit. Nevertheless, some interesting developments occur in location theory at the general equilibrium level under the heading of "central-place theory," a body of theory which has implications for the study of regions that go beyond economics (Chapter 5).

Economic growth, which dominates contemporary economic thought, has had little impact so far on location theory. Nevertheless, some starting points are there, and I will attempt to outline in broad strokes a theory of location for a growing economy (Chapter 7).

SELECTED READINGS

The following are general works on location theory.

Bunge, W., *Theoretical Geography*. Lund: Gleerup, 1962.

Greenhut, M., *Microeconomics and the Space Economy*. Chicago: Scott, Foresman, 1963.

Hagget, P. and Arnold, E., *Location Analysis in Human Geography*. New York: St Martin's, 1965.

Hoover, E. M., *The Location of Economic Activity*. New York: McGraw-Hill, 1948.

Isard, W., *Location and the Space Economy*. New York: John Wiley, 1956.

Lösch, A., *The Economics of Location* (translation of *Die räumliche Ordnung der Wirtschaft*, 2nd ed., 1944). New Haven: Yale University Press, 1954.

Palander, T., *Beiträge zur Standorttheorie*. Uppsala: 1935.

Ponsard, C., *Histoires des Théories Economiques Spatiales*. Rennes: Colin, 1958.

Weber, A., *On the Location of Industries* (translation of *Über den Standort der Industrie*, 1909), Chicago: University of Chicago Press, 1929.

CHAPTER 2

Location of an Economic Activity

A natural starting point for the analysis of locational patterns is to ask where a particular economic activity will be located when the locations of all other activities are given. This is the problem of locational choice.

LOCATIONAL CHOICE

Economic activities rarely occur in predetermined places, but they are generally subject to locational choice (just as choices are required with respect to the timing, the methods, and the scale of production, the input mix, etc.). Technical constraints usually rule out vast areas of any region for any particular activity and reduce the scope of the problem. We may call all locations where an economic activity is technically possible *feasible* locations. If some technical requirement dominates all others, that activity is said to be *oriented* toward it. In this sense mining is raw-material oriented, beer production is water oriented, petroleum refining is energy oriented, the selling of style goods is consumer oriented —and agriculture is, in this sense, soil oriented. However, it should be remembered that not all minerals are actually mined and not all soils that are capable of agricultural production are actually cultivated. While it may suffice in economic geography to list all resource deposits, location theory requires additional considerations in order to explain why particular resources are utilized and to what extent.

Feasibility may depend also on proximity to other economic activities. Certain activities like the testing of atomic bombs require large amounts of empty space. Conversely, sales activities usually require proximity to populated areas. Residential choices depend both on a preference for isolation and privacy on the one hand, and on the availability of human contacts and cultural facilities on the other.

Among all feasible locations for an economic activity there will be some — possibly only one — which is optimal. Optimality for production activity means that profit is maximized. For a consumption activity (residence) it means that utility is maximized; for a public utility, an administrative office, or other object of economic policy it means that "social welfare" is maximized. Whether profit maximization also implies social optimality will have to be examined.

Another question concerns the extent to which optimal locations are realized. In an economy organized on the profit motive, optimal locations will always exert an attraction. It may take a long time for this attraction to overcome inertia, ignorance, and similar forces of friction. Only in a market economy which is competitive throughout is there a compulsion to achieve optimal locations by the threat of elimination of production activities which are not located optimally.

For a monopolist there is no such compulsion, although he pays a price for his nonoptimal choices. The same is true for all consumption activities.

Thus in all cases but that of the competitive firm, there may exist a discrepancy between optimal and actual locations.[1] Nevertheless, for reasons discussed in general economic theory, it is the working hypothesis to suppose that

[1]Lösch, 1954, p. 1. Complete publication information for this footnote and all other footnotes that list just the author and the date of publication can be found in the lists of Selected Readings following each chapter.

economic activities in general and locational choice in particular are governed by the desire to maximize profits or utility.

In every case in a market economy "optimality" as defined will depend on prices of the commodities involved. If all prices relevant to economic activity are independent of location, that is, constant everywhere, then optimality will still depend on proximity to (1) potential customers, (2) similar and competing plants and facilities, and (3) economic activities in general. These will be considered in more detail below.

When factor prices or commodity prices vary with location, their spatial structure is intimately related to transportation costs (see the beginning of Chapter 6). Economies are conceivable in which no transportation occurs — say because it is technically infeasible at a certain stage of development. In that case the possibilities of settlement are severely limited by the requirement that all human necessities be produced locally. Most production activities as we know them involve some inputs or outputs that must be transported. In any case the possibility of removing the output makes it possible to carry out production activities on a scale in excess of local requirements and so to approach more closely the technical optimum.

When a significant part of the inputs or outputs is transported the activity is often called *footloose*. The choice of location is said to be *transport oriented*. Such activities are most clearly in need of locational analysis.

Thus a great variety of situations may arise in locational choice. Location theory does not cover them all equally well, but provides some general tools developed through a closer analysis of certain standard cases.

PLANT LOCATION

Certain production activities are tied to a raw material or to a consumption location. Thus minerals must be extracted where found, crops must be harvested where grown, and buildings be constructed or bridges assembled at points of consumption. But other activities are footloose. As we shall show, the allocation is invariably affected by transportation costs. Here transportation cost is understood in the widest sense, including costs of shopping trips or of communication.

No Transportation Costs

In the special cases where transportation costs of products or of inputs are negligible the meaning of the profit objective is modified and the locational problem is simplified according to the scheme in Figure 2.1.

		Output Price	
		Uniform	Varying
Input Price	Uniform	*Location indifferent*	*Maximum revenue*
	Varying	*Minimum cost*	*Maximum profit*

Figure 2.1. Objectives of Firms Seeking
Optimal Location

Geographically uniform input prices in a region not otherwise perfectly homogeneous are possible only when the input is available everywhere locally at constant production (extraction) cost (1) because no special resources are used and those resources required have the same opportunity cost everywhere (an altogether unlikely event) or (2) because transportation costs are negligible. Uniform product prices exist only in the second case or (3) when close substitutes have uniform prices because their transportation costs are negligible.

Now locations offering maximum revenue will be close to consuming industries or in the consumer goods case close to households and away from other plants of the industry. The revenue maximization objective will therefore tend to disperse the plants of an industry. (For an exception through external economies see Chapter 6, section on pricing in spatially separated markets.) Costs, on the other hand, may operate in two different ways. If inputs are locally dispersed, the plants will have to locate away from each other to secure cheap sources of supply. If inputs are localized, all plants will be attracted to one or a few locations offering the most favorable cost conditions. This is invariably true if the industry uses special resources. But it may happen even when no special resources are used. Thus, a labor-intensive industry can be attracted to locations of unemployed, abandoned, and cheap labor (and become thereby labor oriented). Such labor reservoirs have occurred in remote mountain valleys settled by an immobile population. Historically, toys, textiles, and musical instruments have been produced there, often under the putting-out system. In locations of "heavy industries" there is often available cheap female labor which can then attract labor-intensive industries that use unskilled or semiskilled labor. (An example is the jewelry industry of Rhode Island.)

Constant Production Costs

Suppose next that transportation costs of output are not negligible and that production costs are the same everywhere. In that case the problem is one of maximizing sales revenue net of the costs. In a homogeneous region — with constant population density — the optimum location is then one which is "farthest removed" from the location of any competing plant. (This will be pursued further in Chapter 3 in the section on free entry.) When production costs vary somewhat among locations, the optimum location of an additional plant will be away from other plants at more expensive production sites. The criteria are that (1) the market area be of sufficient size and (2) the increase in production cost be less than the costs of transporting the product from any cheaper production site already occupied by a competitor.

When neither output prices nor input prices are sufficiently uniform to cause the revenue or cost motive to predominate, then the optimal location is that of maximal profit.

General Case

When the given prices of commodities are completely arbitrary, very little can be said about the optimum location of a plant. For each location one can determine a gross profit function which depends on the prices of inputs and outputs. With this profit must be compared the opportunity cost of the location as reflected in the rent for that site offered by competing activities. That site for which profit after rent is maximal is then the optimum location.

For more definite results consider an economy extended along a line (a coastline or valley way), and suppose that the proportions of inputs and outputs are fixed through technological coefficients. Then the gross profit function is a weighted sum of input and output prices. Suppose furthermore that input and output prices are never constant but increase or decrease at the rate of transportation cost as one moves from one end point of the line to the other. Then the maximum of the profit function occurs at an end point of the line. (This is true even when some prices are increasing, so long as some prices are decreasing in such a way as to keep the gross profit function constant.) If there are certain breaks in the price pattern such that, say, an input price is rising up to a point and falling thereafter, then the maximum of the profit function may occur at an interior point, and this will necessarily be such a turning point in some input or output price. After rent, however, any feasible point may turn out to be optimal. This indicates the role of rents in allocating sites to competing activities (this topic will be discussed in Chapter 4).

These considerations may be extended — with some caution — to a two-dimensional region. The optimum location of an activity converting an input into an output with fixed proportions is either at a point of minimal input price or of maximal output price.

ONE INPUT AND ONE OUTPUT

Consider now the case where production consists of processing one transportable input into a transportable output. The case where the input is available locally at constant cost was considered above (as constant production costs). Of particular interest are the following two situations:

1. The input is localized, that is, only available at special points, so-called resource deposits.
2. The input is available everywhere at constant costs but must be collected from an extensive area.

In the first case suppose production decreases the weight and/or bulk of the input, as it does in mineral refining or smelting, coal coking, etc. The processing plants cannot locate profitably away from raw materials deposits. An exception occurs if the capacity of a deposit is below the minimum efficient size for such plants. Then raw materials from several resource deposits must be collected before processing becomes economical. This occurs, for instance, in oil refining. (For problems involving several material deposits see the section below on localized inputs.)

If, on the contrary, production increases weight and/or bulk then the optimal plant location is at consumption locations (local markets) or at the center of a consumption area, for it is cheaper to ship the input than the output. Only significant differences in processing cost could cause a shift away from consumption locations to points of cheap processing cost.

Inputs must be collected from an extensive area in many industries which process agricultural commodities such as in dairying, sugar refining, cotton ginning, wool combing, log cutting, tanning, etc. Plants will seek locations of maximal supply area, that is, as far removed as possible from competing plants. This is analogous to the case of the sales territory when production costs are constant and production is localized.

Usually such processes reduce bulk and weight. The minimum supply area is determined by the minimum scale of operation. In selecting points of maximum distance from other plants of the industry, plants will maximize both supply and market area. Typically the market area is the larger one. If not, outside supplies must come in. Then ports of entry are points where the input is available at relatively or absolutely minimal cost, and these will also be optimal locations for some plants.

SEVERAL LOCALIZED INPUTS

This is the classical plant location problem formulated and analyzed by Launhardt[2] and by Weber.[3]

If several resources are localized, the location of a plant involves new considerations. The following simple model catches the essence of this problem: Suppose that production of a good requires two resources as inputs. There is a single resource "deposit" for each resource and a single market for the product. For example, the market may be von Thünen's "central city" (see below), the product may be pig iron, and the inputs coal and iron ore, each found at a particular point outside the central city. (Limestone, a necessary ingredient in pig iron production, is considered here to be a free good.) Let one ton of iron require 1.7 tons of iron ore and 1.8 tons of coal. Assume that processing costs are the same at all locations. The optimal location would then be the one where transportation cost is minimal, and the locational choice is said to be "transport oriented." According to legend, Gary, Indiana, was planned by U. S. Steel to minimize transportation costs.

If the choice of production sites is restricted to the three given locations, then the coal mine would be best. If as a result ore cars were hauled back empty from the coal mine site, then by lowering the freight rate on coal hauled to the

[2]W. Launhardt, "Der beste Standort einer gewerblichen Anlage," *Zeitschrift des Vereins deutscher Ingenieure* (1882).
[3]Weber, 1929.

ore site, iron production at the ore deposit could be made competitive to that at the coal mine, although more weight is now moved per ton of delivered product. (But since empty ore cars must be moved anyway, the extra cost of hauling ore in them is small.) One can even locate production at all three points in such proportions that there is never an empty haul.

In general, when this plant is just one of many users of the transportation system, economies of back haul play a minor role. The greatest saving in transportation cost is then achieved by locating the plant at that point where total ton-mileage of haul is minimized. Typically, this is a point in the interior of the triangle spanned by the three given points. Let the input of resources A and B per unit output be w_A and w_B, all measured in weight units. Assume constant input coefficients, that is, no increase or decrease in input cost with the scale of production. If production takes place at distances r_a, r_b, r_c from the three given locations, respectively, we seek to minimize transportation cost per unit output: $w_A r_a + w_B r_b + 1\, r_c$.

Mathematical analysis [A][4] shows that the optimal location is uniquely determined by the following condition shown in Figure 2.2.

Draw connecting lines from the unknown location L to locations A,B,C, and consider them as lines of force. The forces are the weights w_A, w_B, 1. The necessary and sufficient condition for the optimal solution at an interior point is that the three forces be in equilibrium. A simple graphical method was developed by Pick[5] to find this equilibrium point [B].[6]

This condition asserts that the closer a location is, *ceteris paribus*, to a given location, the greater is the weight to be hauled to or from there. In fact, if this weight is sufficiently

[4]See Mathematical Notes at the end of the chapter.
[5]Weber, 1929, pp. 225–228.
[6]This has been further developed by Harold W. Kuhn and R. E. Kuenne, "An Algorithm for the Weber Problem," *Journal of Regional Science*, Vol. 4 (1962), pp. 21–23.

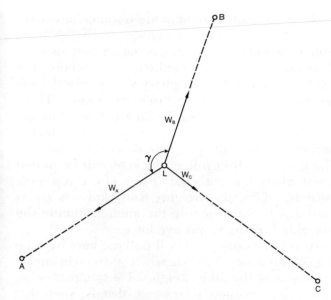

Figure 2.2. Optimal Plant Location Under
Transport Orientation

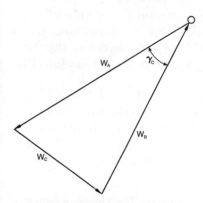

Figure 2.3. Weberian Triangle

large, the optimal location is right at the resource or market location.

The problem of minimizing transportation cost may be solved by an analogue device credited to Varignon.[7] Let three rollers be placed on the periphery of a circular device, in locations corresponding to the three given ones. Three pieces of string are tied by a single knot and weights are attached to the ends of the strings in proportion to the weights that are moved in the problem. When the strings are put over the corresponding rollers the knot will be pulled into that point where the potential energy of the system is minimal, that is, where the weights hang down as far as possible; and this is equivalent to the minimization of the distances weighted by the respective forces.

If one force is large enough, it will pull the knot right up to one roller. This is always the case when one weight equals or exceeds the sum of the other weights. Thus, in particular, production which is weight increasing, that is, such that output weighs more than all inputs taken together, should always take place at the point of consumption; it should be "market oriented."[8]

The same model may be used to solve the following problem of locating a transportation network. Let A,B,C be three points to be connected by a road network. The dollar cost (including construction and maintenance) per mile of highway is a per annum, the dollar cost of transportation per vehicle mile is b. The expected total traffic between the three points is respectively V_{AB}, V_{BC}, V_{CA} vehicles per annum (Figure 2.2).

The per mile cost of roadway and traffic on LA, say, is then $a + b(V_{AB} + V_{CA})$ and correspondingly for the two other highways. The optimal location of the junction is where the three forces are in equilibrium. Of course, this is not the only configuration possible. For sufficiently large volumes of

[7]Weber, 1929, p. 227.
[8]For a critique of Weber, see S. R. Dennison, "The Theory of Industrial Location," *Manchester School of Economics and Social Studies*, Vol. 8 (1937), pp. 23–47.

traffic it is economical to have direct roads between all three points.[9]

The principle of the equilibrium of weights considered as forces still applies, and the analogue device still works when there are more than two inputs and more markets, provided the quantities to be shipped to the various markets are fixed. This is the case, for example, for joint products sold in different markets. As long as none of the given locations is interior to the regions spanned by the others, the equilibrium remains unique. Otherwise, several equilibria are possible, although only one represents the true transportation cost minimum. The equilibrium of forces is still necessary but no longer a sufficient condition. The various topological configurations must be tried out, and no "marginal criterion" is possible that can distinguish among them.

The assumption that processing costs are everywhere equal may also be relaxed. Suppose that locations of equal wage rate are connected by isocurves. They may be thought of as level curves of constant wages.[10] A new force may now be introduced, representing the rate of increase of the wage rate. This force will pull in that direction where the decrease is greatest—opposite to the "wage gradient." The minimum production and transportation cost is then at that point where this force is balanced by the transportation cost forces, that is, the pull of weights. Thus, cheap labor competes with the other resource deposits as a drawing force for plant locations.

Let us now drop the assumption of a single market and of single deposits for each resource. If economies of scale are absent and if from each deposit resources may be extracted at constant unit cost, then the previous model applies to

---

[9]Martin Beckmann, "On the Optimal Location of Highway Networks," in *Quantitative Geography, Part I*, William L. Garrison and Duane F. Marble, eds. (Evanston, Ill., Northwestern University Press, 1967) pp. 95–119.

[10]Spatial isocurves have been extensively investigated by Tord Palander, *Beiträge zur Standorttheorie* (Uppsala: Almquist and Wiksell, 1935).

each plant of the industry. Each market will be served by one plant, using resource deposits nearest to that market (or rather to that plant) and located where the transportation forces are in equilibrium.

If resource extraction capacities are limited, then those where demand exceeds capacity due to favorable location will, under perfect competition, sell resources at a premium above extraction cost. A given market is then served by the resource deposits supplying its plant at minimum delivered price. Due to capacity limitations of resources, several plants may be necessary to supply one market. Formally we have a linear programming problem combining transportation and production activities (Chapter 6).

With economies of scale in production the nature of the location problem is changed. Only in exceptional cases will each market require and be able to support a separate plant; and the question then is: Which markets should form the sales territory of which plant, and how many plants should there be?

Given the location of plants there is always of course a linear programming solution to the problem of the optimum allocation of markets to plants that is determined by marginal conditions. But the determination of the optimum *number* of plants is a more difficult problem. Marginal conditions alone are no longer sufficient, since alternative configurations must now be tried out.

Suppose, for instance, that a single plant is required. The Weber-Launhardt theory will permit many solutions, all of which represent local cost minimums. There is no short cut to finding the global minimum. It is possible to formulate the problem as a linear program in integers, provided one approximates this continuous variable problem in terms of a selection among finitely many discrete points.[11] To calculate the actual solution is in general still a formidable task.[12]

[11]William J. Baumol and Philip Wolfe, "A Warehouse Location Problem," *Operations Research*, Vol. 6 (1958), pp. 252–263.

[12]M. L. Balinski, "Fixed Cost Transportation Problems," *Naval Research Logistics Quarterly*, Vol. 8 (March, 1961); Leon Cooper, "Location-

However, some programs make use of intuitive ideas to set up a search process or "heuristic program" for locating, for example, a set of warehouses.

1. Most geographical locations are not promising sites for a regional warehouse; locations with promise will be at or near concentrations of demand. . . .
2. Near optimum warehousing systems can be developed by locating warehouses one at a time, adding at each stage of the analysis that warehouse which produces the greatest cost savings for the entire system. . . .
3. Only a small subset of all possible warehouse locations need be evaluated in detail at each stage of the analysis to determine the next warehouse site to be added.[13]

LOCATION IN A NETWORK

So far we have assumed that transportation cost is either proportional to geometric distance or is at any rate a function of this distance. This is true only when the transportation network will be constructed along with a plant and if construction costs per mile are equal everywhere; or it is true as an approximation when the network is very dense.

Often choice of a site is restricted to points on (1) a given transportation network or to points (2) located close enough to be connected to the network at reasonable cost.

The location problem[14] is then reduced to a one-dimensional one. In simple cases the network is just a

Allocation Problems," *Operations Research*, Vol. 11 (1963), pp. 331–343; M. A. Efroymson and T. L. Ray, "A Branch-Bound Algorithm for Plant Location," *ibid.*, Vol. 14 (1966), pp. 361–368; E. Feldman, F. A. Lehrer, and T. L. Ray, "Warehouse Location under Continuous Economies of Scale," *Management Science*, Vol. 12 (May, 1966), pp. 670–684.

[13]Alfred A. Kuehn and Michael J. Hamburger, "A Heuristic Program for Locating Warehouses," *Management Science*, Vol. 9, No. 4 (July, 1963), p. 645.

[14]Herbert Gülicher, "Einige Eigenschaften optimaler Standorte in Verkehrsnetzen," *Schriften des Vereins für Sozialpolitik*, New Series, Vol. 42 (1965), pp. 110–137.

single line (in a valley) or a closed circle (an island with settlements along the coast).

Single Input

In the point input-point sales case, the plant will be attracted to that location from or to which the larger weight must be moved; that is, weight-increasing production will be attracted to the point of consumption, weight-decreasing production to the raw material site. For extensive supply and sales territories the same is true, the necessary changes having been made. In an otherwise homogeneous region, the market and supply areas will be concentric; in a two-commodity world (one agricultural product, one industrial product) they will also be coextensive.

When several inputs are involved, analysis along the same lines as above shows that minimizing transportation cost still entails a comparison of forces represented by the weights of resources and products pulling in the various directions. Along an edge of the network these forces can pull only in two opposite directions. The result will be that the location is pulled into a vertex. This is done at no increase or decrease of cost even when by chance the two forces are equal. In this way the special attractiveness of transportation centers or at any rate of junction points is revealed.

At the optimal vertex the forces channeled along the diverging routes must again be an equilibrium. This means that moving the plant a little way along any of the routes increases transportation cost. Hence weights moved along any edge must be less than total weight moved along all the other edges which join this vertex. In general, several vertexes may satisfy this condition and yet total transportation costs may differ. Thus the equilibrium of forces is once more a necessary but not a sufficient condition of optimality.

MATHEMATICAL NOTES

[A]

Let X_i, Y_i, be the coordinates of point i where $i = A,B,C$; and let X,Y be the coordinates of the plant location L. Total transportation cost is

$$T = \sum_{i=1}^{3} w_i \sqrt{(X_i - X)^2 + (Y_i - Y)^2}$$

For an interior minimum the partial derivatives with respect to X and Y must vanish.

$$\sum_i w_i \frac{X - X_i}{\sqrt{(X_i - X)^2 + (Y_i - Y)^2}} = 0 \tag{1}$$

$$\sum_i w_i \frac{Y - Y_i}{\sqrt{(X_i - X)^2 + (Y_i - Y)^2}} = 0 \tag{2}$$

Now

$$w_i \frac{X - X_i}{\sqrt{(X_i - X)^2 + (Y_i - Y)^2}}$$

is the X coordinate of a vector of length w_i pointing from i to L. Equation (1) means that the X component of the composite weight forces vanishes. The two conditions together mean that the composite vector vanishes, that is, that the three weight forces are in equilibrium.

[B]

The basic idea is that the three forces may be arranged as a triangle (Figure 2.3) and that the angles of this triangle (e.g., γ_c) are complements of those at the equilibrium point L (i.e., $\gamma_c = 180° - \gamma$). One then constructs the circles which are the loci of those angles (e.g., γ) above their respective base (AB).

SELECTED READINGS

Greenhut, M., *Microeconomics and the Space Economy; the Effectiveness of an Oligopolistic Market Economy*. Chicago: Scott, Foresman, 1963.

————, *Plant Location in Theory and Practice*. Chapel Hill: University of North Carolina Press, 1956.

Hoover, E. M., *The Location of Economic Activity*. New York: McGraw-Hill, 1948, pp. 27–46.

Lösch, A., *The Economics of Location* (translation of *Die räumliche Ordnung der Wirtschaft*, 2nd ed., 1944). New Haven: Yale University Press, 1954, pp. 1–24.

Meyer, W., *Die Theorie der Standortwahl*. Berlin: Duncker und Humblot, 1960.

Weber, A., *On the Location of Industries* (translation of *Über den Standort der Industrie*, 1909). Chicago: University of Chicago Press, 1929. Pick's original work appears in the Mathematical Appendix of the 1929 edition, pp. 225–228.

CHAPTER **3**

Location of an Industry

In analyzing the location of an industry we begin with the short-run problems of how markets are allocated among plants whose locations are given and consider then the long-run problems of location proper.

CLASSIFICATION OF MARKET AND SUPPLY AREAS

The locational distribution of an industry is the classical problem of location theory. However, it turns out that no single answer can be given to this problem, for upon analysis this problem is found to consist of a complex of situations which require rather different approaches.

In analyzing plant locations, two possible tendencies have emerged: Plants seek to locate away from each other at a maximal distance or on the contrary they are attracted to each other. In the latter case the cause may be that favorable conditions are present in only one or a few places; or it may be that the concentration of several plants of an industry has created a market there which—due to uncertainty on the part of consumers about the location of suppliers and the range of goods offered—does not exist elsewhere.

These two tendencies give rise to different locational

patterns at the industry level: dispersal or concentration. A more detailed classification is achieved by the scheme of Miksch[1] (with subdivisions added), which runs along the following lines:

Four basic situations may be distinguished according to the space requirements of producers and the population density of consumers

1. Producers and consumers concentrated at point locations and in point markets
   1a. Single point
   1b. Multiple points

2. Producers concentrated in points, consumers extended through an area (market area)
   2a. Single point
   2b. Multiple points

3. Consumers concentrated, producers dispersed (supply area)
   3a. Single point (central city)
   3b. Multiple points

4. Both producers and consumers distributed through an area: continuously extended market.

Which of these cases is realized by any given industry is of course itself to be explained by location theory. The market structure (monopoly, oligopoly, monopolistic competition, perfect competition) and the period under consideration (short run versus long run) also create distinctions.

Case 1a — producers and consumers concentrated in a single location — is the spaceless economy usually assumed in general economic analysis. Case 1b underlies the classical linear programming model of transportation to be considered in Chapter 6. Case 2a and 2b will be considered in the section below on market areas. Case 3a is the subject of Chapter 4 (the von Thünen model); case 3b is similar to it. Case 4 will be considered briefly in Chapter 6.

---

[1] L. Miksch, "Zur Theorie des räumlichen Gleichgewichts," *Weltwirtschaftliches Archiv*, Vol. 66 (1951), pp. 5–50.

We now turn to the standard case: an industry which produces a single product from resources which are available everywhere at uniform cost. As we shall see, in such a homogeneous setting, the location problem is not to pinpoint locations but to determine the distances which separate the locations of these economic activities.

Market Areas

The question is: Given that the plants of an industry are located where they are, how are their sales determined, other things being equal? In particular, how are the buyers of the entire region allocated among the sellers? When are there well-determined subregions — to be called market areas — such that each is supplied by one and only one plant? We observe first that sales depend on the all-inclusive price that a demander pays. This price depends in turn on the system of pricing used by the industry (for more detail see the section below). Here and throughout, unless stated otherwise, we shall assume that producers quote a fixed price at the factory gate — a mill price — and that the transportation cost is borne by the buyer. Also (unless stated otherwise) transportation cost is assumed to be proportional to distance and weight.

Under these assumptions there will exist at any given point of the region one plant from which the good is secured at minimum cost to the buyer, that is, the delivered price is minimal. At some points, which in fact must lie on certain curves, delivered price from *two* sources is smallest and equal. Finally there will be points for which three sources are equally cheap. Only in exceptional cases can there be points where prices from four or more plants are equal and minimal.

In this sense there are well-defined market areas characterized by the fact that in a market area one plant is the cheapest supplier. Whether consumers always choose to buy from the cheapest source (even when the product, as here, is assumed to be homogeneous) is another question.

As Launhardt[2] has observed, when transportation cost is less than proportional to distance then a low-priced seller will undercut the price of a higher-priced seller at points beyond some distance. In that case the market area of a cheap supplier breaks up into several parts or else surrounds that of his higher-priced competitors.

With proportional transportation costs this is impossible, and only the following two situations can arise: Either a producer is undercut by a competitor at his own plant location, and then his market area is nil or he is the cheapest supplier at his plant site and, by continuity, in an entire area surrounding it. If this market area is surrounded by market areas of other suppliers, it can never include any points beyond this boundary.

It is possible that market areas are open in some directions since they are not bounded by market areas of competitors (Figure 2.3, where the price of the three suppliers is assumed to be the same). There are well-defined boundaries between the market areas; in fact, these are straight lines. How far outward do the market areas extend?

Obviously, as far as a demand exists, it is customary to disregard the possibility that sales vanish because of a vanishing population. Rather the border line is defined by the condition that delivered prices reach the critical level, where demand falls to zero. This price level is usually assumed to be the same for all locations. This means that an open market area is bounded in any case by a circle whose radius defines the critical delivered price.

Adjacent market areas, on the other hand, are separated by boundaries along which delivered prices from the two supply points are equal. Along the boundary itself delivered price will of course vary. In the case of equal mill prices the boundary is a straight line, the normal bisection of the line connecting the two supply points.

When mill prices differ the boundary is a hyperbolic arc (since a hyperbola is the curve for which distances from two points differ by a constant amount). An example will be con-

[2]W. Launhardt, *Mathematiche Begründung der Volkswirtschaftslehre* (Aalen: Scientia Verlag, 1963), p. 160 (reprint of edition of 1885).

sidered in the von Thünen model, where a satellite of the central city appears as a second supplier.

In the case of three suppliers with equal mill price the lines separating the market areas will meet in one point, dividing the entire market into three wedge-shaped areas. Generally, when f.o.b. prices are equal, the market areas of suppliers are separated by a polyhedral net of boundary lines. If three suppliers have different f.o.b. prices, their market areas will be pair-wise separated by hyperbolic arcs which curve around the more expensive location. Hence, delivered prices are equal for a pair of suppliers on the boundary line separating the market areas. It follows again that the intersection point of two boundary lines is also on the third boundary. Hence, wherever two boundaries meet they will meet a third.

In the case of suppliers with different mill prices a net of market areas will be formed which is bounded by arcs of hyperbolas that curve around the more expensive of any two suppliers they separate. Any two boundary arcs that intersect always meet with a third boundary in this intersection point, thus forming a corner point (see Figure 3.3, below).

It follows that a plant can always extend its market area in all directions by lowering its mill price. In an industry where mill prices are equal for all plants, a change in transportation costs does not change market areas except those which are not bounded by competing market areas.

Market areas play an important role in the competition of coal mining districts (Ruhr versus Silesian coal in prewar Germany), of oil fields (Gulf versus West Coast oil fields), and in delimiting the hinterlands of ports.[3]

ALTERNATIVE ALLOCATION OF SALES

Transportation cost may not play the decisive role in determining sales as assumed so far, because the costs are rel-

[3]Lösch, 1954, pp. 295–298.

atively small, making price differences among alternative suppliers also small; or because the products are not homogeneous and consumers value their qualities in such a way that these quality differences are not always compensated for by price differences. In these cases sales territories will overlap, but the competitive position of a product still declines with distance, partly because of transportation cost and partly because of communications (including advertising) cost. Thus colleges will tend to attract a smaller percentage of the student population as distance from them is increased.

Various formulas have been proposed to catch this "interaction at a distance." The formulas best supported by theoretical arguments and empirical tests are variants of the "principle of gravity." When applied to sales, this principle asserts that demand for one product as a percentage of total demand for products of the industry is at any given point proportional to total sales of that product in all locations and is inversely proportional to the distance of the point from the supplier [A].

In more general formulas distance is replaced by a power function of distance (or of transportation cost = economic distance) or by some other monotonically increasing function.

A similar idea underlies the "intervening opportunity hypothesis" — in fact an exponentially declining distance factor — and the "Law of Retail Gravitation."[4]

PRICE POLICY

The position of producers in various given locations is determined not only by the extent of their market areas but above all by their sales potential in these areas. It is therefore necessary to consider the revenues — and profits — obtainable under different methods of pricing.

We shall assume that producers costs consist of a fixed cost and a constant average variable cost (unit cost).

[4]W. J. Reilly, *The Law of Retail Gravitation* (New York: Reilly, 1931).

Let demand be proportional to population times a linear demand function (which is assumed to be independent of location).

Monopoly

Consider first a single producer—or several producers so far apart that their market areas will not touch or overlap under any conceivable price policy. To begin with, in order to simplify the analysis, we may again assume that the market extends along a line.

Price Discrimination

Now the largest monopoly profit will be forthcoming if the producer can discriminate perfectly between his customers according to their location. Let $p(r)$ be the price to be charged buyers at distance r. A simple calculation [B] shows that the best discriminatory price increases at half the rate of transportation costs: The monopolist charges a monopolistic mill price, $p_0 = (a + bc)/2b$, which depends on the demand function and on marginal cost only, and he absorbs half the freight to the buyers' location.[5] This result is independent of the distribution of population. It means that the nearby customers whose demand is relatively inelastic are charged relatively more, in relation to cost, than the distant customers.

The market area will extend to the same distance as if the mill price was set at marginal cost and full transportation costs were charged, and the critical price is reached at the point where demand is zero (Figure 3.1). This is obviously the largest distance over which one would want to sell under any system of pricing (call it R), since beyond that distance price could never cover marginal cost of production and of transportation. Note that marginal cost need not be constant.

[5]H. W. A. Singer, "Note on Spatial Price Discrimination," *Review of Economic Studies* Vol. 5 (1937), pp. 75–77.

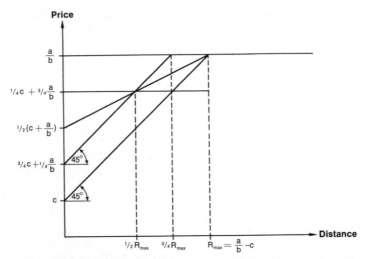

Figure 3.1. *Alternative Price Policies*

NOTE: Figure 3.1 compares the price-distance relationships for uniform, mill, and discriminatory pricing. The rate of transportation cost is assumed to be unity. Marginal costs in Figure 3.1 rise along a line of 45° slope. The horizontal line at level a/b indicates the maximum price — that for which demand is zero. Uniform delivered price appears as a horizontal line at $(1/4)c + (3/4)(a/b)$. The market extends to $(3/4)R_{max}$ the maximal market radius, for at that point marginal cost = price.

Under mill pricing the price line starts at $(3/4)c + (1/4)(a/b)$ and has a 45° slope. The market radius is again $(3/4)R_{max}$. While costs are covered at every point, this is the distance at which demand falls to zero.

Only under discriminatory pricing does the market extend as far as R_{max}, that is, to the point where the maximum price just covers the marginal cost of production and transportation. Note that at $(1/2)R_{max}$ the same price is charged under all three systems.

In fact, even if returns to scale in production are increasing throughout, causing marginal costs to fall everywhere, an optimal size of the firm exists which minimizes the average cost of production plus transportation, provided the market is large enough. This follows from the fact that the marginal cost of transportation increases proportionally to output if the region is homogeneous and even more than proportionally when population density falls with increasing distance.

Mill Pricing

Suppose next that firms quote a mill price either to avoid administrative complications in connection with discrimination or because discrimination is illegal. We now assume a constant population density.

Again consider first an isolated firm. With the previous assumptions about demand and costs it is found [C] that the profit-maximizing mill price is three-fourths marginal cost plus one-fourth maximal demand price. At the mill this price lies below the mill price under perfect discrimination but above the marginal cost price. It follows that the sales radius is reduced to three-fourths of the maximum sales radius R. (See Figure 3.1.)

The proportions are different and the price is higher when it is assumed that a greater population density prevails at the mill than in the remaining area.

Uniform Pricing

Consider next the case of a monopolist fixing a unique delivered price — the alternative that is found most frequently in practice when transportation costs are not a large part of total costs.

The possibility arises that the monopolist will refuse to deliver beyond a certain distance — at the point where price just equals marginal cost plus transportation cost. If, on the other hand, government regulation compels the monopolist to fill all demand, this will of course influence — that is, raise — his optimal price.

Suppose, however, that the monopolist is free from this restriction, that demand is uniformly dense, and that the market is unlimited. Then, a straightforward calculation shows [D] that in contrast to the case of a uniform mill price, the optimal price is now equal to one-fourth of the marginal production cost plus three-fourths of the maximal price (that is, the price at which demand falls to zero). Notice that transport cost does not enter directly. Again whether the monopolist covers all costs depends on the size of his fixed cost. In any case, the optimal uniform delivered price is above the optimal mill price. Notice that a uniform delivered price is also a form of price discrimination.

Is a uniform delivered price or a mill price more profitable? Under the assumptions made here, they turn out to be equally profitable: The disadvantages of diminished control over transportation cost that are inherent in uniform pricing are made up by larger sales at the longer distances, that is, where most of the consumers are. Of course profits are even higher under discriminatory pricing.

Which system is more advantageous to the consumer? To this no general answer can be given: Under mill pricing those near the source are better off, while under a uniform price system the distant consumers are in a more favorable position.

Duopoly

As in oligopoly analysis generally, spatial oligopoly is best approached through a study of its most elementary case, that of duopoly.

Discriminatory Pricing

If other firms encroach on our sales territory the optimal policy will be to meet their price at a point below the perfectly discriminatory price

$$\frac{1}{2}\frac{b}{a} + \frac{1}{2}c + \frac{1}{2}kr$$

and to demand the perfectly discriminatory price where we can charge it. This leads to the pattern shown in Figure 3.2. Up to a certain point we will be charging the same price as if the competitor were not there, and beyond we are just meeting or slightly undercutting the competitor's price.

If he retaliates, the zones of contention will become larger; eventually a situation may emerge where no uncontested area remains: The rival has to meet our price on his territory just as we will meet his on our own territory. Prices then show the paradoxical pattern of decreasing as one moves away from any supplier to a trough midway between sup-

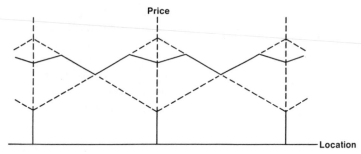

Figure 3.2. *Spatial Price Discrimination*

pliers. This situation can be an equilibrium but only when fixed costs of all participants are covered. Otherwise, this is just one stage in a price war which may end by forcing some of the participants out of the market and/or by their reaching a collusive agreement on market sharing of the type to be discussed below.

Mill Pricing

When a second plant using a mill price system is close enough to undercut its competitor from some distance on, the first plant will be forced to reduce its price, since it always pays to extend the market area somewhat. Here we assume the firm to act on the supposition that the competitor's price is fixed.

It can be shown that the own mill price is an increasing function of the rival's given mill price in the relevant range. As a result of mutual adjustments of prices a Cournot duopoly equilibrium[6] is reached in which further price changes are not profitable any more. In this equilibrium the hypothesis that the rival's price remains unchanged has at last come true. It is remarkable that in a spatial economy a Cournot equilibrium exists also for price adjustment and

[6]A. Cournot, *Researches into the Mathematical Principles of Wealth* (1838), trans. by N. T. Bacon (London: Macmillan, 1897), ch. 7.

not only for quantity adjustments (which we have not considered here). Whether this type of equilibrium allows firms to survive because they cover their fixed costs depends on their proximity to each other, since this will determine the size of their market areas. This duopoly need not be stable: If the optimum number of firms is smaller—say one firm rather than two—and if no legal or psychological barriers exist to a combination, this is not a stable situation, for a single monopolist will do better.[7]

Uniform Delivered Prices

Suppose that under uniform pricing market areas overlap. We may recall that market areas were defined as those within which firms are willing to deliver, that is, where they can recover marginal cost of production and transportation. Suppose in fact that prices of two competitors are equal. Then by an infinitesimal price reduction a firm could gain a finite increase in sales by expanding its market territory to the limit at an infinitesimal cost of reducing revenues from its previous sales. Here we have in fact the situation of the Edgeworth-Bertrand oligopoly model. Therefore the following possibilities arise:

1. Mutual price cutting until the level of marginal cost of the (second) cheapest producer is reached
2. Price cutting to be followed by a price rise up to the monopoly point because capacity limitations of the lowest-price firm or distance leave a market for the others
3. Some agreement to be reached for price fixing

This may take the form of an explicit agreement among all or of informal price leadership by a leading firm. Competition is then shifted to service and product quality variation, that is, product differentiation. The price leader

[7]See, for example, D. Dewey, "Imperfect Competition No Barrier to Efficient Production," *Journal of Political Economy*, Vol. 66 (1958), pp. 24–33.

may choose the price that maximizes his own profit. A price set by a coalition would involve bargaining of the type analyzed in the theory of n-person cooperative games.[8] It appears, however, that spatial considerations as such do not enter into the determination of the solution set or of the choice of a particular solution.

Collusive Oligopoly

An alternative to price cutting and to settling at a Cournot equilibrium is some agreement on price fixing. Under the system of mill pricing or discriminatory pricing two extreme possibilities are:

1. Uniform minimum mill prices. Here the prices are fixed and the market areas, the exclusive territories of the various sellers, are determined indirectly. An alternative is to fix the market areas and to allow each firm to choose its own mill price. However, when customers can buy more cheaply outside the territory to which they have been allocated, this becomes a source of potential trouble with the public and the government. It may in fact not be possible to set prices in such a way as to keep a cheaper supplier out of one's market area.

2. The basing point or "Pittsburgh-plus" system. The mill price of one location determines *delivered price* at all locations regardless of the plant from which delivery is made. Of the various consequences we mention the following four:

The market area of mills at the basing point is larger than that of any other location and may include the entire national economy unless the critical price is reached inside the national boundaries.

From any other location the market area extends only to points where price covers marginal costs of production and transportation. This is again a hyperbolic area, for the differ-

[8]John von Neumann and Oscar Morgenstern, *Theory of Games and Economic Behavior*, 3rd ed. (Princeton: Princeton University Press, 1953) and Walter Isard, "Game Theory, Location Theory, and Industrial Agglomeration," *Regional Science Papers*, Vol. 18 (1967), pp. 1–11.

ences of distances from the plant and the basing point must not exceed a certain constant which depends on the basing point price and the marginal cost of production [E].

There is no incentive for avoiding wasteful allocation of plants to markets or even cross hauling.

An artificial incentive is set up to locate plants at the basing point: Only from here is the entire market accessible, and moreover basing prices are often determined by the cost structure at the basing point. Such artificial geographic concentration is economically undesirable. The best-known examples have occurred in the steel and cement industries,[9] but this system is now illegal almost everywhere.

Price Fixing and Market Allocation

The entire region is split into territories allocated to the various firms as exclusive market areas. Transportation cost may be considered but need not be decisive [F]. Therefore the allocation tends to be wasteful, since the same demand could be met at a saving in production and/or transportation costs. The most profitable price may then be set by each producer independently according to the principles of monopoly, although transportation cost will exert a moderating influence.[10] Examples are the various international cartels which divide the world market into exclusive spheres of influence.[11]

Monopolistic Competition

Consider the case where the product of a single firm competes with similar but not homogeneous goods. Suppose that the other producers are widely diffused at a roughly constant population density. The competitive position of the firm's product will depend on the distance of customers from the location of the producer. We assume that it is described by

[9]Frank Fetter, *The Masquerade of Monopoly* (New York: Harcourt, Brace, & World, 1931).
[10]Greenhut and Pfouts, 1957.
[11]Stocking and Watkins, 1946.

a gravity formula [G]. Let transportation costs be negligible. It can be shown that the optimal price is determined by the same principles as in nonspatial monopolistic competition and that the profit is proportional to a certain variable which measures the "average distance of a location from population," the so-called potential of population.[12]

Perfect Competition

Consider finally the case where customers buy from the cheapest supplier regardless of distance. This may happen, say, in a big city, where consumers do not value the time costs of shopping trips. This case is the closest approximation to perfect competition in space, provided the number of firms is large. It is apparent that prices will be equalized and will be brought down to the level of marginal cost of the marginal supplier. The same result will come about if customers, while not willing to travel to the ends of the entire region, are willing to disregard costs of shopping trips to the second- or third-closest plant whenever it charges a lower price than the nearest plant.

Perfect competition may arise also when transportation costs are important but not sufficient to outweigh production cost advantages of a single best location at which all producers are concentrated, provided that there are enough of them. A well-known example is the concentration of hat manufacturers in Danbury, Connecticut, before World War II.

GENERAL PRINCIPLES OF RELOCATION

Suppose that some change has occurred in the location of the neighbors of a given plant. As the plant wears out, its replacement may be established at a more favorable loca-

---

[12]G. K. Zipf, *Human Behavior and the Principle of Least Effort* (Cambridge, Mass.: Addison-Wesley Press, 1949); William Warntz, *Toward a Geography of Price* (Philadelphia: University of Pennsylvania Press, 1959).

tion. When customers pay transportation costs (in the form
of shopping trips) and demand is independent of that cost,
then the optimum location is one which secures for the plant
the largest area within which it is the closest supplier. Consider the largest convex polyhedron spanned by other plants
as vertexes such that no further plant is inside the polyhedron. (These polyhedra will be quadrangles, pentagons,
hexagons, etc.) Inside this polyhedron a point is sought for
which the area bounded by normal bisectors to the lines
connecting that location with the corner points is at a maximum (Figure 3.3). An analogue device for this construction
is as follows: let balloons be centered at the given vertexes
and let them be blown up to a certain pressure. We now
introduce a balloon inside the polyhedron area and adjust
air pressures until the boundaries are normal bisectors. The
central balloon will adjust its location so as to maximize the
volume occupied. In a regular polyhedron the optimal location is of course the center.

If all plants are allowed to relocate simultaneously then
they will arrange themselves in a regular pattern — a regular
lattice. The same result is approximated when adjustments
take place successively many times over. In fact among the
three possible regular configurations the only "packing" that
is stable in the sense of being densest is the hexagonal
lattice (the others being triangular and square). The boundaries of market areas form a regular honeycomb.

Duopoly

Special considerations are needed when the number of
firms is so small that oligopolistic conditions prevail rather
than those of monopolistic competition assumed so far. The
classical problem is that of Hotelling's two ice-cream vendors on a beach: Let people be spread out at uniform density.
They will buy ice cream at a constant rate from the nearest
supplier regardless of actual distance. Given that the location of one vendor is temporarily fixed, where will the other
locate?[13]

[13]Hotelling, 1929.

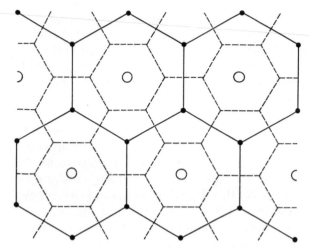

Figure 3.3. *Range of Stable Market Areas Under Free Entry*

Obviously right next to the first one on that side which faces the larger market. Through numerous repetitions they will gradually move to the center of the beach. This is of course a wasteful location from the customer's point of view who must on the average walk greater distances than if the vendors had located at the quartile points.

In a two-dimensional market with a small number of suppliers there will be a corresponding tendency to cluster around the center, for each location away from the center is dominated by one closer to the center. The situation becomes unstable as the number of plants increases: If a few plants are dispersed, the advantage of the center is sufficiently reduced to bring about general dispersion along the lines described below.

FREE ENTRY

When profits are made in an industry this is a signal for new firms to enter. In a uniformly populated region, the best point of entry is at the center of the largest potential market area.

Under a system of mill pricing, an additional plant will reduce the demand—at a given mill price—for the product of any plant whose market area is contiguous to that of the new plant. The new plant thus shifts the demand curves at the neighboring plants in a downward direction. As this is repeated, the demand curves will eventually just barely exceed or be tangential to the average cost curves. The industry has then no room for further plants. It has reached an equilibrium under monopolistic competition with a maximum number of plants—a larger number in fact than is consistent with the minimization of average cost of production, since the equilibrium point is on the declining branch of the average production cost curve. When short-run cost consists of a fixed cost and a constant marginal cost the entire long-run average cost curve is of course declining.

But what about the average of production plus transportation cost? Now minimization of production plus transportation costs requires an output below that for which production cost alone is minimized, for average transportation cost is rising throughout so that the sum of both can be at a minimum (i.e., stationary) only when average production cost is falling (Figure 3.4). Now under monopolistic competition the equilibrium output is also less than that for which average production cost is minimal, unless the established firms are overselling in an effort to prevent entry of new firms.[14] But it would be an accident if the two outputs coincided so that monopolistic competition would tend to minimize average total cost.

Under uniform delivered pricing, from a certain point on a new plant can enter only when it sets a lower price. Whether this price is met or undercut by the other firms or not, adjacent plants will find their market areas reduced. Price competition forces prices down to that level where the marginal cost of production plus delivery to the farthest point of the market area are just covered.

How does the minimum area required to sustain a plant

[14]Donald Dewey, "Imperfect Competition No Barrier to Efficient Production," *Journal of Political Economy*, Vol. 66 (1958), pp. 24–33.

under uniform pricing compare with a minimum area under mill pricing? Since receipts from sales to points inside the borders of the market area exceed marginal cost, firms have a greater return per unit area and can therefore be compressed into smaller areas under long-run equilibrium. This is borne out by calculations for one-dimensional market areas (not given here).

By the same token discriminatory pricing allows firms to survive on the smallest market areas possible. Of course average prices are lower under uniform delivered prices and lowest under mill pricing. In a sense, the density of plants in long-run equilibrium is inversely related to the level of consumers' satisfaction.

Under free entry, the long-run situation is the same regardless of short-run agreements about price fixing and/or market areas. It depends, however, as we have seen, on the method of charging for transportation cost (uniform delivered price versus mill price, etc.).

Does long-run equilibrium imply that all points are included in (at least) one market area? Or to put it differently: Are all market areas compressed to the shape of hexagons?

Under mill pricing it is conceivable that minimum-sized market areas must be so large that the critical price level is exceeded at the corners. In that case the market area is a hexagon whose corners have been cut off by circles on which prices attain their critical level.[15]

Under uniform pricing it is much more likely that prices are forced down to the point where marginal cost of production plus transportation to the corners are not covered. The same argument would apply to discriminatory pricing. However, as a rule the densest packing of firms in a model of free entry in long-run equilibrium shows the hexagonal pattern of market areas first proposed by Lösch.[16]

So far we have assumed that free entry achieves in the end the densest packing of market areas consistent with the survival of plants. (A biological analogue would be a densest

[15]Mills and Lav, 1964.
[16]Lösch, 1954.

settlement by predatory animals that permits them to survive on their hunting preserves.) However, this is an extreme case. Long-run equilibrium is consistent with a smaller density of plants, as I shall now show.

Assuming a regular hexagonal pattern of plant locations, what is the critical distance of plants such that new plants have just room to enter?

The best chance is offered at the center of the triangles formed by three adjacent plant sites. Let a be the minimal distance, that is, the distance under the densest packing. A simple calculation (see Figure 3.3) shows that the critical distance is $C = a\sqrt{3}$. This means that any hexagonal pattern with a plant distance between $a + 0$ and $a\sqrt{3} \approx 1.732a$ is stable under free entry.

The minimal distance a must itself be calculated from the population density, the demand curve, and the costs of production and transportation. Of course the method of pricing also matters (see above). Now long-run equilibrium need not even result in a regular, for example, hexagonal, pattern, although under relocation such regularity has a tendency to emerge (see Relocation, above).

The above calculation rests on the assumption that a new firm has as good a chance of survival as an existing one. If its chances are smaller, the range of indeterminacy is increased. If a new firm introducing a more modern plant can in fact force out several existing firms, then nothing short of the densest packing has the property of long-run stability.

OPTIMAL DISTRIBUTION OF PLANTS

Among the stable hexagonal patterns of different mesh width, which is the optimal one? Lösch has argued that it is that one which maximizes the number of independent "existences," for example, plants, and this means the tightest packing at that minimal distance a which allows the firms to survive on zero profits.[17]

[17]*Ibid.*, p. 96.

Since perfect competition under free entry is consistent with various sizes of the market area, as we have seen, no definite answer comes from that direction. Also, various systems of pricing must be compared.

Given a uniform delivered price, say, the level of consumption will be the same everywhere. The social optimum is then achieved by maximization of the consumption levels, that is, the minimization of unit cost. This is not the same as minimizing cost per plant. But since the total area is given, it amounts to minimizing cost per area. As the market area of a plant is expanded, the overhead (fixed) cost per unit output falls but the average transportation cost per output rises. The minimum is found where the slopes of the two curves are equal and opposite (Figure 3.4).

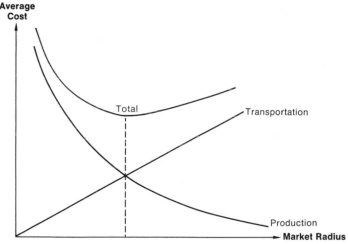

Figure 3.4. *Average Cost Curves*

If the firm's cost curve is defined as the sum of production and transportation costs, then the neoclassical theory of the firm can be applied. Notice that the *marginal* cost curve is rising throughout, even though marginal cost of production is constant under our present assumptions. Eventually, combined marginal cost will be rising no matter how fast the marginal cost of production is decreasing, that is, regardless of any economies of scale in production. When some cost of plant is fixed, the *average* cost curve is in any case initially decreasing, and in view of the above-mentioned properties of the marginal cost curve average cost reaches its minimum for a finite output. Thus economies of scale in production are always consistent with an optimum scale of plant.

The optimum delivered price is the minimum delivered price; for as price is lowered so that consumption per area is raised, the average cost per area and the average cost per unit of output both fall, and the average cost minimum is reached in the smallest area possible. Thus the optimum price equals minimum average cost of output for the minimum market area that can be realized. It is associated with the maximum number of plants that will enter under free entry provided that entering plants consider the prevailing uniform market price as given.

Of course the lowest price can be achieved only when the market areas are circular. Such a system of plants would leave the corners between any three circles unsupplied — and these corners will occupy approximately 0.092 of the total area [H].

Now the optimal radius of a circular market area and the optimal price are so related that at the market boundary, price just covers marginal cost of production and transportation. The optimal price itself is the smallest positive root of a certain fourth-order polynomial [I].

If the condition is imposed that all locations are to be supplied, then the pattern of market areas must consist of one of the three types of regular polyhedrons — triangles, squares, hexagons — that form a regular network. Among these, hexagons are optimal. To see this consider the average distances between supplier and consumers. These may be calculated by straightforward integration. The results are shown in Table 3.1.

Of all systems of regular market areas that will cover a plane completely, the hexagonal one is most efficient in the sense of minimizing the distance to be covered between supplier and demander per unit area when demand is given.

Table 3.1 *Average Distances Between Supply and Demand*

Type of Market Area	Equal Radii	Equal Areas
Circular	$\dfrac{2}{3} R$	$\dfrac{2}{3} r$
Hexagonal	$\left(\dfrac{1}{3} + \dfrac{1}{4} \log 3\right) R \approx 0.6079\,R$	$0.6685\,r$
Square	$\left(\dfrac{\sqrt{2}}{3} + \dfrac{1}{3} \log \tan \dfrac{3\pi}{8}\right) R \approx 0.5407\,R$	$0.6776\,r$
Triangular	$\left(\dfrac{1}{3} + \dfrac{1}{6\sqrt{3}} \log \tan \dfrac{5\pi}{12}\right) R \approx 0.4600\,R$	$0.7154\,r$

This understates its advantage, since a more efficient market system in this sense allows prices to be lower, consumption to be higher, and the density of firms to be larger, so that actual average distances differ by even more than this table indicates.

For a hexagonal market area it is no longer true that the optimal price and width are such that at the farthest boundary point (the radius R) marginal costs are still covered; this is true for some special points on the boundary, but the cost of reaching the farthest corners exceeds the price. The optimal price is again a root of a certain fourth-order equation, and the price is necessarily higher than under a regime of circular market areas, where some consumers are left out [J].

Under mill pricing when entering firms consider price as given they will tend to bring down average production cost to the absolute minimum, as is shown in the general neoclassical theory of long-run equilibrium of the firm. But this disregards the costs of transportation, and so there is a systematic bias which leads firms to have market areas which are too large from a social point of view. This is understandable, since transportation costs are external to the firm; and the competitive process necessarily disregards transportation costs and thus fails on the average to minimize the sum of production and transportation costs. For the same reason the more refined objective criterion of maximizing the aggregate consumer's surplus minus total cost is also not realized under mill pricing in a spatial market. This is perhaps understandable, since this type of competition is "monopolistic" rather than "perfect."[18]

Optimal Number of Farms

The determination of optimal supply areas is simpler than that of market areas if it can be assumed that the areal density of supply is given. Take as an example the determination of the optimum number of farms producing a certain crop commodity. Assume a rectangular road network. Economic distance is the sum of the distances in the two principal directions of the road system. Each farm requires a certain supply area. For simplicity consider a single crop which is grown by a given technology so that the yield per area is also given and constant. What is the optimum number of farms, or, since total area is given, what is the optimal size of a farm? For technical reasons (equal length of furrows) the farm land must be assumed to have a square shape with sides running in the principal directions of the road system. The length of a "section" turns out to be related in a simple way to the technical data of agricultural production [K].

If the working capacity of a family is less than required by this section length a, then the farm size must be reduced. But this reduction increases the cost of output per acre. In the same way, *mutatis mutandis*, the optimum size and number of villages may be determined in the case when farmers choose to live in villages rather than on the land. Optimum sizes of supply areas have also been calculated by Bos.[19]

INHOMOGENEITIES

In a plain without distinguishing features, with local variations in climate and fertility but otherwise homogeneous,

[18]Cf. also Mills and Lav, 1964.
[19]H. C. Bos, *Spatial Dispersion of Economic Activity* (Rotterdam: University Press of Rotterdam, 1965), pp. 25–36.

population density will vary from location to location. Even if, initially, resources and population are all distributed at a uniform density, as soon as plants of some industry have been located, population density will show local variations. Even when no trade of intermediate commodities takes place — an output of one industry being an input to another — an industry producing consumers' goods will be drawn to the locations of plants of other industries simply because of the higher population density at those locations. Of course this tendency is reinforced by the exchange of intermediate products among industries.

Let us denote all locations of one or several plants from other industries as "centers." It may happen that the market at a center is large enough for several plants of this industry. In the absence of oligopolistic practices preventing free entry, as many plants will locate as is consistent with competitive or monopolistically competitive equilibrium, whichever prevails.

Even when only one plant is located in a center, the size of the surrounding market area is less than calculated for a homogeneous region. In a purely homogeneous region the density of plants was shown to increase as a power function of degree 2/3 with population density.

Inhomogeneity may also take the form of differences in production costs at different locations. At a cheap production site, the firm will command a larger market area than its competitors. If it is protected against the entry of new firms, say, because the market does not support more than one plant, the extra profit is the firm's rent. This rent will fall to the landowner, since the competition from potential entrants will drive land rent to that level.

When plants of several industries are competing, the site will go to the plant whose advantage is greatest there as reflected in its ability to pay rent. The relationships between competing types of land use and rent are of particular importance and interest in the case of agricultural production, to which we now turn.

[A]

The formula is

$$D_{ij} = c_i \frac{S_j}{r_{ij}} \tag{1}$$

where

D_{ij} = demand at location i for products of supplier j.
S_j = total sales of supplier j.
r_{ij} = distance from i to j.
c_i = a factor of proportionality.

Actually if total demand at i is D_i we have from

$$D_i = \sum_j D_{ij} = c_i \sum_j \frac{S_j}{r_{ij}}$$

$$c_i = \frac{D_i}{\sum_j \frac{S_j}{r_{ij}}}$$

The formula (1) gives the distribution of total demand D_i among competing products j

$$D_{ij} = D_i \frac{\frac{S_j}{r_{ij}}}{\sum_k \frac{S_k}{r_{ik}}}$$

Here the distance variable r_{ij} may also enter as a power function r^{α}_{ij}. For instance in Reilly's "Law of Retail Gravitation" $\alpha = 2$.

[B]

Let $g(r)$ be population density; $a - bp$, demand function; p, price; c, marginal production cost; k, unit transportation cost per unit distance. Then profits obtained from customers at distance r are $g(r)(a - bp)(p - c - kr)$. Differentiation with respect to r yields $p = (a/2b) + (c/2) + (kr/2)$. Observe that the price at the mill $p_0 = (1/2)(a/b) + (1/2)c$ is the mean value of the maximum demand price a/b and of marginal cost c.

[C]

Optimal mill price in a circular market area: Let p be mill price; c, marginal cost; $a - bp$, demand curve; r, distance; $k = 1$ transportation cost per unit distance; R, maximal distance $= (a/b) - p$; G, gross profit before fixed cost. Now

$$G = (p - c) \int_0^R 2\pi r[(a - bp) - br]\, dr$$

$$= (p - c)\left[\frac{1}{2b^2}(a - bp)^3 - \frac{b}{3b^3}(a - bp)^3\right]$$

Ordering terms we have

$$G = \frac{1}{6b^2}(p - c)(a - bp)^3$$

Taking the derivative with respect to p and setting it to zero

$$(a - bp)^3 - (p - c)(a - bp)^2\, 3 = 0$$

from which

$$p = \frac{1}{4}\frac{a}{b} + \frac{3}{4}c$$

In a one-dimensional market the optimal price turns out to be

$$p = \frac{1}{3}\frac{a}{b} + \frac{2}{3}c$$

[D]

Optimal delivered price: Using the same notation as in note [C] but letting p stand for delivered price, we have demand, $a - bp$; profit per unit sold at distance r, $p - c - r$; the sales radius R is determined by $c + R = p$. Total profit is

$$G = \int_0^{p-c} (p - c - r)(a - bp)\, 2\pi r\, dr$$

Integrating, we obtain

$$G = 2\pi(a - bp) \left[(p - c) \frac{(p - c)^2}{2} - \frac{(p - c)^3}{3} \right]$$

$$G = \frac{\pi}{3}(a - bp)(p - c)^3$$

Setting the derivative with respect to p equal to zero, the optimal price, p is calculated:

$$p = \frac{3}{4}\frac{a}{b} + \frac{1}{4}c$$

For a one-dimensional market the optimal delivered price turns out to be

$$p = \frac{2}{3}\frac{a}{b} + \frac{1}{3}c$$

[E]

Let p_0 be the base price and c the marginal production cost at a plant. Consider a point to which the plant wants to ship. Let r_0 be its distance from the basing point; r, its distance from the plant; k, transportation cost per mile. Price received by the plant is $p_0 + r_0 k$; cost is $c + rk$. The market area is therefore limited by the condition that $c + rk \leqq p_0 + r_0 k$ or $r - r_0 \leqq (p_0 - c)/k$ and the boundary line occurs where the equality sign applies. It defines a hyperbola.

[F]

When market territories are allocated, the optimal price can be calculated rather simply, since it does not affect the size of the market area. Let the notation be as in note [C], and let $q(r, \varphi)$ be the population density at the point (r, φ). Then profit is given by

$$G = (p - c) \iint_{\substack{\text{fixed} \\ \text{area}}} (a - br)\, q(r, \varphi) r dr\, d\varphi$$

provided price does not exceed the cutoff point a/b anywhere. Now

$$\frac{dG}{dp} = \iint (a - bp - br)\, q r dr\, d\varphi -$$
$$(p - c)\, b \iint q(r, \varphi)\, r d\varphi\, dr = 0.$$

From this

$$\iint (a - 2bp - br + bc)\, q r dr\, d\varphi = 0$$

$$p = \frac{\iint (a - br + bc)\, q r dr\, d\varphi}{2b \iint r dr\, d\varphi}$$

$$= \frac{1}{2}\frac{a}{b} + \frac{1}{2}c - \frac{1}{2}\bar{r},$$

where $\bar{r}$ denotes the average distance of shipment. Thus prices at the mill will be lower the larger the average distance $\bar{r}$ of points in the market area from the supply center. On the other hand, the average price paid by consumers including transportation cost is independent of the shape of the market area and its size, that is, it is always equal to $(1/2)c + (1/2)(a/b)$. (Here the weights are by area, not by amount of consumption.)

Average distances for various regular areas are shown in Table 3.1.

[G]

Let $q(r, \varphi)$ denote the density of customers located at a point with polar coordinates (r, φ). The plant is located at $r = 0$. Now $a - bp = A_0$ is the demand per person for this product in the absence of competing products. Let A_i denote the attractiveness of the ith competing product. Let $r_i(r, \varphi)$ be its distance from location (r, φ). Then by the gravity formula the firm's sales to location (r, φ) will be

$$S = A_0 \iint \frac{q(r, \varphi) \, r^{-\alpha} r \, dr \, d\varphi}{A_0 \, r^{-\alpha} + \sum_i A_i \, r_i^{-\alpha}}$$

Under the stated assumptions, the "strength of the competition"

$$\sum_i A_i \, r_i^{-\alpha}$$

is approximately the same everywhere, equal to A, say. Now sales are

$$S = A_0 \iint \frac{q(r, \varphi) \, r \, dr \, d\varphi}{A_0 + A \, r^\alpha}$$

Since A is large we may approximate

$$S \approx \frac{(a - bp)}{A} \iint \frac{q(r, \varphi) \, r \, dr \, d\varphi}{r^\alpha}$$

In particular if $\alpha = 2$ (as in the Law of Retail Gravitation) the integral becomes what is known as the potential of population, P. Now profits are

$$S \, (p - c) = \frac{1}{A} \, (a - bp) \, (p - c) \, P$$

and maximal profits, with $p = (1/2) \, (a/b) + (1/2)c$, are proportional to P, as are sales.

[H]

The area of the triangle spanned by three plant locations at distances $2R$, respectively, is $R^2\sqrt{3}$. The area of three sectors of the circle, each measuring 60 degrees, equals

$$\frac{3\pi R^2}{6} = \frac{\pi}{2} R^2$$

The unsupplied area as a percentage of the area of the triangle is therefore equal to

$$1 - \frac{\pi}{2\sqrt{3}} = 0.092$$

[I]

With the notation of note [C] profits before fixed costs from sales in a circular territory of radius R are

$$\int_0^R 2\pi \, q(a - bp) \, (p - cr) \, r \, dr \tag{1}$$

If the firm covers its fixed costs f, this integral must equal f. Integrating we have

$$2\pi \, q(a - bp) \left[(p - c) \frac{R^2}{2} - \frac{R^3}{3} \right] - f = 0 \tag{2}$$

This equation determines p implicitly as a function of R. To find the optimal R we take the implicit derivative dp/dR and require it to vanish. This yields

$$R = p - c \tag{3}$$

as expected. At the optimal market boundary the firm just covers its marginal cost. Substituting (3) in (2) we obtain a fourth-order equation in p

$$(a - bp) \, (p - c)^3 = \frac{3f}{\pi q} \approx 0.955 \, \frac{f}{q} \tag{4}$$

If the fixed cost f is sufficiently small, then this equation can be solved; in fact it has in general two real roots, of which the smaller is to be taken. This root lies in the range

$$c < p < \frac{a}{b}$$

and it increases with f and decreases with q. This is shown by implicit differentiation as well as the observation that since it is the smaller root the left-hand side is rising there.

If f is too large the commodity cannot be sold at any price that would cover production cost; it must then be imported.

[J]

Let $\bar{r}(R)$ denote the average distance of points in a hexagon of side length R to the center. Profits are then given by

$$q \iint_{\substack{\text{hexagon of} \\ \text{radius R}}} [p - c - \bar{r}(R)] \, (a - bp) \, dx \, dy - f$$

Since the integrand does not depend on r any more, the integral equals the integrand times the area, and the area is $(3/2) \sqrt{3} \, R^2$. Substituting for $\bar{r}(R)$ from Table 3.1 we have

$$\left[p - c - \left(\frac{1}{3} + \frac{1}{4} \ln 3 \right) R \right] (a - bp) \, q \frac{3}{2} \sqrt{3} \, R^2 - f = 0 \tag{5}$$

Taking the implicit derivative dp/dR and setting it to zero we obtain

$$R = \frac{2(p - c)}{1 + \dfrac{3}{4} \ln 3} \approx 1.096 \, (p - c)$$

It follows that the marginal cost of supplying the remotest point exceeds price

$$c + R = c + 1.096 (p - c) = 1.096 p - 0.096 c > p$$

since $c < p$.
Substituting in (5) we obtain for p the fourth-order equation

$$(p - c)^3 (a - bp) = 0.960 \frac{f}{q} \tag{6}$$

A comparison of the coefficients in (5) and (6) shows that p is higher under a hexagonal system than under a circular one.

When demand is independent of price, $b = 0$; then equation (2) may be solved

$$p = c + \sqrt[3]{0.960 \frac{f}{aq}}$$

Here the root term denotes the margin of price over short-run marginal cost of production.

A comparison of equations 4 and 6 shows that a hexagonal market system leads to a 17 percent increase of the margin of price over marginal cost of production.

A similar calculation for the square yields an equation

$$(p - c)^3 (a - bp) = 0.9868 \frac{f}{q} \tag{2'}$$

When demand is independent of price the increase in the margin over that for a circular area is approximately 32 percent; for a triangular market area the increase in the margin over that for a circular area may be calculated to be 55 percent.

[K]

Let the side length of this square be a. Total distance traversed on the farm annually is then ma^3, where m is the number of trips to each piece of land required per year

$$4 \ m \ \int_0^{a/2} \int_0^{a/2} (x + y) \ dx \, dy = ma^3$$

Let the fixed cost of a farm be f, the trip cost per mile be k. Then to minimize cost per area it is required that

$$kma^3 + \frac{f}{a^2} = min$$

from which

$$km = \frac{2f}{a^3} \qquad a = \sqrt[3]{\frac{2f}{km}}$$

SELECTED READINGS

Ackley, G., "Spatial Competition in a Discontinuous Market," *Quarterly Journal of Economics*, Vol. 56 (1942), pp. 212–230.

Clark, J. M., "Basing Point Methods of Price Quoting," *Canadian Journal of Economics and Political Science*, Vol. 4 (1938), pp. 477–489.

Fetter, F. A., "The Economic Law of Market Areas," *Quarterly Journal of Economics*, Vol. 38 (1924), pp. 520–529.

Greenhut, M., "The Size and Shape of the Market Area of a Firm," *Southern Economic Journal*, Vol. 19 (1952–1953), pp. 37–50.

Greenhut, M., and Pfouts, R. W., "The Pricing Policies of a Spatial Monopolist," *Metroeconomica*, Vol. 9 (1957), pp. 155–166.

Hoover, E. M., "Spatial Price Discrimination," *Review of Economic Studies*, Vol. 4 (1937), pp. 182–191.

———, *The Location of Economic Activity*. New York: McGraw-Hill, 1948, pp. 47–66.

Hotelling, H., "Stability in Competition," *Economic Journal*, Vol. 39 (1929), pp. 41–57.

Hyson, C. D., and Hyson, W. P., "The Economic Law of Market Areas," *Quarterly Journal of Economics*, Vol. 64 (1950), pp. 319–327.

Lösch, A., *The Economics of Location* (translation of *Die räumliche Ordnung der Wirtschaft*, 2nd ed., 1944). New Haven: Yale University Press, 1954, pp. 105–116.

Machlup, F., *The Basing-Point System*. Philadelphia: Blakiston, 1949.

Mills, E. S., and Lav, M. R., "A Model of Market Areas with Free Entry," *Journal of Political Economy*, Vol. 72 (1964), pp. 278–288.

Moses, L., "Location and the Theory of Production," *Quarterly Journal of Economics*, Vol. 72 (1958), pp. 259–272.

Smithies, A., "Optimum Location in Spatial Competition," *Journal of Political Economy*, Vol. 49 (1941), pp. 423–439.

Stigler, G. J., "A Theory of Delivered Price Systems," *American Economic Review*, Vol. 39 (1949), pp. 1143–1159.

Stocking, G. W., and Watkins, M. W., *Cartels in Action*. New York: Twentieth Century Fund, 1946.

Stouffer, S. A., "Intervening Opportunities: A Theory Relating to Mobility and Distance," *American Sociological Review*, Vol. 5 (1940), pp. 845–867.

CHAPTER **4**

Allocation of Land

VON THÜNEN'S THEORY

From industrial activities that use little land we now turn to agricultural activities that use land extensively. In fact the location problem for agricultural activities centers on the competition for land use. The classical analysis of the allocation of land to competing agricultural activities is that of von Thünen, which we will now develop.

Consider a very large town in the center of a fertile plain which does not contain any navigable rivers or canals. The soil of the plain is assumed to be of uniform fertility which allows cultivation everywhere. At a great distance the plain ends in an uncultivated wilderness, by which this state is absolutely cut off from the rest of the world.

This plain is assumed to contain no other cities but the central town and in this all manufacturing products must be produced; the city depends entirely on the surrounding country for its supply of agricultural products.

All mines and mineral deposits are assumed to be located right next to the central town.

The question now is: How under these circumstances

will agriculture be developed and how will the distance from the city affect agricultural methods when these are chosen in the optimal manner?[1]

The problem may be described in graphical terms (Figure 4.1). Let the horizontal axis measure the radial distance from the city and the vertical axis net revenue per acre. By net revenue we mean revenue (price of product times quantity) minus labor cost (and fertilizer and other direct cost) and minus transportation cost. For any given product net revenue at the city is easily calculated from the given product price, the input coefficients for this product, and the price of labor and other inputs.

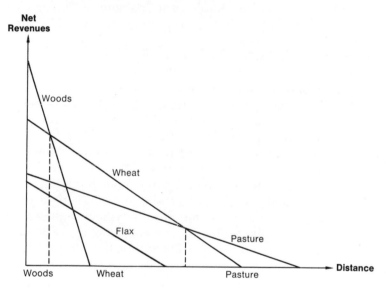

Figure 4.1. von Thünen Rings

As we move away from the city, net revenue decreases at the rate of transportation cost for the acre-product [A].

[1]Johann Heinrich von Thünen, *Der isolirte Staat in Beziehung auf Nationalökonomie und Landwirtschaft* (Stuttgart: Gustav Fischer, 1966), pp. 11–12. (This is a reprint of the 1826 edition.)

For any product net revenue is therefore described by a downward sloping line whose slope equals transportation cost per acre-product per unit-distance. A farmer located at a certain distance from the city and owning a given acreage will maximize profits by choosing the product which at that distance has maximum net revenue and by growing this product exclusively.

Under modern conditions of agricultural technology, production must be interpreted to mean a sequence of products, a "rotation" (as it was by von Thünen). The crucial assumptions are that a finite number of possible activities (products or rotations) exists; that technological coefficients are fixed; and that prices are fixed. These assumptions make the problem an early example of a "parametric linear program."[2] Specialization in one activity at a given distance means a "corner solution."

We note the following: Certain products may not be grown at any distance, if their price at the center is too low. Two products, which are not identical in technological respects, will be grown only in a "hairline area" — a border strip between exclusive zones of cultivation. The areas of cultivation — von Thünen's rings — follow upon each other in the order of increasing transportation cost per acre-product. Thus, as distance from the city increases, the individual products or the yields or both must become lighter. Transportation costs are not just a function of weight but should include deterioration in transit as well. Thus emerges the typical sequence of truck gardening, milk production, cereals, grazing areas, and forests. Animals are raised in an outer ring, then shipped and fattened closer by (see Processing of Agricultural Output, below).

The upper contour of the net revenue lines represents maximum net revenue or rent per acre. The rent is thus seen to decrease with distance from the city at a rate which is constant in each ring and decreases from ring to ring. This contour is therefore "convex." Eventually, at the outer border of cultivation, rent falls to zero.

[2] G. B. Dantzig, *Linear Programming and Extensions* (Princeton: Princeton University Press, 1963), p. 241.

SIMPLE EXTENSIONS

The von Thünen model explains a number of important facts about agricultural production locations—in a strikingly simple way; in particular the fact of agricultural specialization even in the absence of climatic and fertility differences, and the decrease of rent with distance from markets. Moreover this is a fertile model capable of extension and modification in various ways. Some of these will now be indicated.

Quantitative Demand

To determine the price level and the extent of cultivation of this "isolated state," consider the size of the urban population and the quantities demanded of various food stuffs and other agricultural products (fibers) as given. Then prices must be found such that the required quantities are forthcoming. The order of cultivation is again given by the ranking of weight products per acre. The quantities of products can then be translated into acreages and the distance found where the various rings begin. However, care must be taken that the maximal distance required is technologically attainable, that is, that the inputs for transportation do not equal or exceed the resources of the economy. Obviously, at any given state of technology there exists a maximal size of the supply area of the city, and hence, a limit to the size of the city itself. Before this maximum is reached, however, other forces will usually cause a multiplication of cities and a decrease in the size of supply areas (see Chapter 7).

If the isolated state is hemmed in by the "surrounding wilderness" and the population grows to such an extent that the available land area is taken up by the more intensive production activities, then some agricultural products will have to be imported.

The type of agricultural import depends on comparative advantage—it need not be that of an outer zone. However, if land is scarce it is likely that imports will consist of the more land-intensive products, that is, those produced in the more distant rings.

Effect of Wage Differences

Wages may vary with distances from the city. This will affect labor costs of growing the various crops, and it will cause the slopes of the net revenue curves to differ from the transportation costs. Thus, if the wage level falls with increasing distance from the city, the net revenues will be tilted in an upward direction, causing rents to fall less rapidly than transportation costs of area products and the area of cultivation to be larger. But the principal conclusion remains unaffected, namely, that production occurs in specialized zones or rings. The type of agricultural import depends on comparative advantage—it need not be that of the outer zones.

Urban Rings

The von Thünen model may be applied within the city itself for an explanation of its residential structure. The product is now "housing of people." The methods are high-rise apartment houses, multistory row houses, free-standing two-story houses, ranch type homes, etc. For each type of housing there exists a price (or rent per month) that one is willing to pay when this housing is available at the very center of the city (that is, next to the central business district). This price decreases with distance from the central business district at a rate which includes not only the money cost but also the cost of increased travel time. (This may be offset in part by greater proximity to the open country.) Per acre this transportation cost is roughly proportional to the number of persons being housed on it. Hence, the types of residential housing will be arranged in order of decreasing density per area as one moves away from the central business district.[3]

[3]Wingo, 1961 and Alonso, 1964.

Waterways, roads, or railroads will make transportation cheaper along some routes. The curves of equal distance or transportation costs ("isotims") are then no longer circles. In the case of three roads converging on the city and on the assumption that transportation costs on the road are half of those outside, the isotims are triangles whose vertexes lie on the trunk roads. If the transportation cost ratio is less than one-half, the isotims are star-shaped (Figure 4.2); if not, they approach hexagonals.[4]

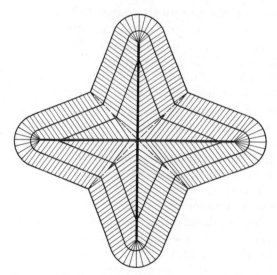

Figure 4.2. *Isotims and Flows at an Intersection of Roads*

PROCESSING OF AGRICULTURAL OUTPUT

Consider now the possibility of converting two agricultural products into a third, say, young beef cattle (the output of

[4]On isotims, cf. Tord Palander, *Beiträge zur Standorttheorie* (Uppsala: 1935).

grazing land) and corn into fattened beef and, finally, beef carcasses. Assume that the conversion process requires no land and has constant returns to scale at any level.

If the economy had two zones before—grazing land and corn land—a third zone will now be added. If transportation over a unit-distance of a beef carcass costs less than transportation of the amount of corn feed required per carcass, the fattening will take place in the outer part of the corn belt; otherwise, in its innermost part.

Generally, the principles of location of production activities without space requirements are these: If the product is bulkier or heavier than total inputs, then the product is never shipped but produced at the place of consumption. (If transportation cost of the product is equal to that of all inputs, production may take place anywhere between the location of the innermost input and the place of consumption.) Otherwise, production takes place in an extensive zone where the input with the most interior location is grown, and this zone adjoins the outer boundary of this input belt.

Even though the conversion process itself is assumed to require no space, it is carried out in an entire area, since it is attached to the production of one input. Additional space requirements by the conversion process would serve to decrease the intensity of the production process per unit-area. In that case the activity of raising and converting the input would give rise to a new and more distant ring.

Processing of agricultural products may also take place with increasing returns to scale—in fact this is the typical situation. If the output is bulkier and/or heavier than the inputs, then this process will be carried out in the central city. Otherwise "plants" will be set up at the center of supply areas outside the central city, assuming that the scale of the economy exceeds the optimum scale of plant. The product will be shipped from these plants to the city, and these plant sites will be potential nuclei for secondary cities (see Chapter 5 below).

The principles described above apply to production for export, not production for local consumption.

Should "interior products" be exported also to exterior rings? If so then the price of the delivered product would have to include the higher rent in the interior plus transportation costs. Clearly it is cheaper for producers in exterior regions to grow, locally, the products of interior regions for their own consumption although it does not pay them to ship these interior products to the central market.

On the other hand it is uneconomical to produce locally the products of exterior zones: The diagram shows that delivered price per acre-product is below rent. Hence exterior products are never produced in interior zones. We conclude that all agricultural commodities move toward the center; the area of a zone must be large enough to produce exports not just for the city but for all consumers located between itself and the city.

The same principles apply when a second, smaller city appears on the scene; it will import products of all exterior rings (that is, from outside the ring in which it is located) and will in its neighborhood raise all products of interior rings.

The exterior rings will be split into two supply areas. Since product prices are different in the central and in the satellite city, the boundaries will be hyperbolic arcs (see page 28, above).

If a sufficient number of satellite cities appear, the central city may be cut off from some exterior ring(s). These products must then be imported or must be processed in the smaller city before reaching the central city (see Chapter 5 below).

Why a Central City?

Finally, suppose that all production enjoys constant returns to scale. Then, all activities would be extended at a uniform density over an area inherently unbounded, unless some focus were created by other means. With homogeneity of the resource distribution, a city will exist only when at least one service, say government, is localized; this localization may take place because of indivisibilities in itself or in some of its parts and because of the cost of communication or transportation between these parts.

Then, the city which harbors this service will export only this service and collect taxes in kind from the rest of the area. This is a sufficient reason for the generation of a central destination. All other products (and other services) are now either produced at the place of consumption or are assembled in one zone for export to more central zones.

Of course, the central city, having the highest population density, will also have the largest output per area of goods produced for local consumption.

Outward Orientation of Flows; Other Configurations

Suppose that no centralized government services exist but that special resources or products must be imported from abroad. Assume that the country has an east and a west coast and is bordered by impenetrable mountains and deserts along its northern and southern frontiers. Let import activities have constant returns to scale so that they are extended at a uniform density along each coast.

Production of goods from domestic resources will take place in belts whose dividing lines run parallel to the coasts. (Figure 4.3). Production of the most extensive good (the one having the smallest yield in terms of weight per unit-area) now takes place in an interior zone having the lowest rent and smallest population density per area. This zone need not be at the geographical center—it will be farther removed from the coast with the greater trade volume. Nor need it be connected—it may consist of two belts between which there is a true desert, that is, a zone of no cultivation. The coastlines will harbor also all production activities which process imported foreign resources, and cause them thereby to lose weight or bulk.

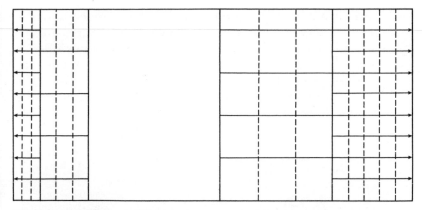

Figure 4.3. *Flows and Zones*

INHOMOGENEITIES

Consider an economy with two products which require specific types of soil. Let this soil occur in two adjacent patches. Then production of each product will extend from the boundary line outward; and rents will decline with increasing distance from the common border, that is, from points of shipment.

Now consider a product requiring both agricultural crops as inputs. Then in the light of the previous analysis production will take place everywhere for local consumption, if there is no loss of weight or bulk in processing. If the product is cheaper to transport than one of its inputs, production will extend through an extensive area of the home ground of that input adjacent to the home ground of the other input.

To summarize, when returns to scale are constant, concentration of production can take place only in response to forces external to this economy: along a borderline when resources are imported from abroad or at a point when indivisible government activities create a focus of consumption. Otherwise they extend through belts which are arranged such that the weight loss per unit-area through a production activity decreases as one moves toward the market, normally, the interior of the country.

All manufacturing activities and those service activities which are not spread out continuously over an area are concentrated in point locations because of economies of scale. Typically these production activities require a fixed or setup cost independent of scale. The implications of this fact for the distribution of production centers will be examined in the next chapter.

MATHEMATICAL NOTE

[A]

Actually von Thünen assumed that transportation was by horse-drawn vehicles and that the horses' feed had to be carried along. Then transportation costs increase with distance in the same manner as for rockets, which must carry their own fuel.

Let c = capacity of the vehicle.

k = rate of feed consumption per unit-distance round-trip.

Then to cover a distance r and return takes up an amount kr of the vehicle's capacity. The payload is $c - kr$. Transportation cost per weight unit carried to distance r is therefore

$$\frac{kr}{c - kr} = \frac{1}{\dfrac{c}{kr} - 1}$$

The maximal distance that can be reached is clearly

$$R = \frac{c}{k}$$

Transportation cost increases sharply near this critical distance: Under von Thünen's transportation technology the supply area of a city and hence the city's size are rigidly limited.

SELECTED READINGS

Alonso, W., *Location and Land Use*. Cambridge, Mass.: Harvard University Press, 1964.

Chisholm, M., "Agricultural Production, Location, and Rent," *Oxford Economic Papers*, Vol. 13 (1961), pp. 342–359.

Dunn, E. S., Jr., *The Location of Agricultural Production*. Gainesville: University of Florida Press, 1954.

Egbert, A., and Heady, E.O., "Regional Programming of Efficient Agricultural Production Patterns," *Econometrica*, Vol. 32 (July, 1964); pp. 374–386.

Henderson, J. M., "The Utilization of Agricultural Land: A Regional Approach," *Regional Science Association, Papers and Proceedings*, Vol. 3 (1957), pp. 99–114.

Hoover, E. M., *The Location of Economic Activity*. New York: McGraw-Hill, 1948, pp. 90–102.

Lösch, A., *The Economics of Location* (translation of *Die räumliche Ordnung der Wirtschaft*, 2nd ed., 1944). New Haven: Yale University Press, 1954, p. 20.

Organization for European Cooperation and Development, *Interregional Competition in Agriculture: Problems of Methodology*. Paris, 1965.

Wingo, L., *Transportation and Urban Land*. Washington, D. C.: Resources for the Future, 1961.

CHAPTER **5**

Central Places

From the analysis of the location of single economic activities we must now turn to the study of several inter-
dependent activities. This will also lead to an explanation of
why cities form in an otherwise homogeneous region.

TWO COMMODITIES

Consider two industries. If their products are unrelated,
each will locate independently in a hexagonal pattern of its
own. If the output of one is used only as an input of the other,
and if their optimal plant size is identical, the two industries may be treated as one. The optimal-sized plant is replaced by an optimal-sized combination of two plants. The
interesting case is that where part of the output of one
industry (A) is used as input by the other industry (B), or
when the efficient plant sizes are rather unequal. As long as
the number of plants in both industries is not too dissimilar,
there will be a tendency for plants of the two industries to
locate together. Suppose that one firm of industry A, at its
most efficient size, produces input for just two firms of industry B at their most efficient size. Then a firm A may locate

at any point on a straight line between two firms B and serve both with the same transportation cost. However, if transportation costs are less than proportional to distance, for example, because of a fixed cost of loading, then it pays to locate next to one firm and ship to the other. Doing so may also increase the potential market. For in equilibrium there will be six firms B (or at any rate several) located as closely as the nearest neighbor B. Firms with horizontal unit production cost will be able to supply all six with equal efficiency. Thus, even when optimal sizes are different, firms of the supplier industry still tend to locate near some firm of the receiving industry. An alternative hypothesis is that an industry will not always locate with other identical industries, but will join clusters of different companies that are located at equal distances.[1] In this way, a much greater variety of types of central places becomes possible, and the principle of strict hierarchy no longer applies.

Conversely, when the number of suppliers is larger, then they must all cluster around receiving plants. Again, with horizontal cost curves, one supply plant will suffice for every receiving plant. (Throughout we assume that processing cost is the same at all locations.) If all transportation is channeled along a rectangular grid of roads, then instead of a supply plant serving seven receiving plants it will serve five: one at its own location and four neighbors. Suppose now that a minimum-size supply plant requires a market larger than five or seven plants of the receiving industry (plus whatever goes to consumers directly within that area). To serve six or fewer additional plants the radius of the market must be increased by a factor of $\sqrt{3}$.

While the "area" served increases threefold, the number of plants served is merely doubled (approximately). This is no paradox. Before there was more unallocated area outside the boundaries of market territories, area that contained no plant location.

[1]In Edwin von Böventer, "Die Struktur der Landschaft," *Schriften des Vereins für Sozialpolitik*, New Series, Vol. 27 (1962), pp. 77–133, in particular, p. 103.

Note that locating away from a receiving plant does not increase the number of receiving plants within a given distance or decrease average transportation cost to them; on the contrary it will raise this cost (Figure 5.1).

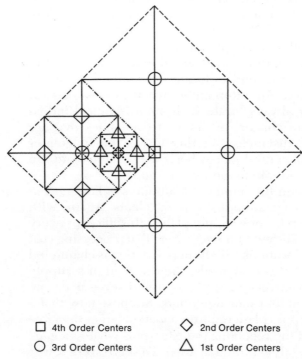

☐ 4th Order Centers   ◇ 2nd Order Centers

○ 3rd Order Centers   △ 1st Order Centers

Figure 5.1. *Nesting of Quadratic Markets*

In a quadratic point lattice, doubling the distance increases the area served fourfold; the number of points served, from five to thirteen (= 1 + 4 + 8).

In any case, the location of supplying firms will occupy a subset of the locations of the receiving firms. The territories of the supply firms will be a union of territories of receiving firms. This is the beginning of a hierarchical pattern of supplier locations.

HIERARCHY MODEL

Let all points of economic activity lie on a square lattice, and let transportation routes form a rectangular network through the lattice points. The basic distance is a. Activities which serve more than one point may have a market radius of $a, 2a, \ldots, ka$. The number of points reached is then as given in Table 5.1.

Table 5.1

Market Radius	Number of Points Within Radius
$1a$	$1 + 4 = 5$
$2a$	$1 + 4 + 8 = 13$
$3a$	$1 + 4 + 8 + 12 = 25$
ka	$1 + 4 (1 + 2 + 3 + \ldots + k) = 1 + 4 \dfrac{k(k + 1)}{2}$

Approximately then, the number of plants served increases as the square of the distance. In a large region with many points there will be room for centers of all levels serving markets of different radius—as long as the products with different market radii are unrelated.

Suppose, however, that a certain product goes to plants which serve markets of radius $2a$. For this product, then, the choice is one between markets of radius $2a, 4a, 6a, \ldots$. The tightest system of distribution centers that can be formed when products are reprocessed or redistributed is one in which the market radii increase in a sequence $a, 2a, 4a, \ldots$ $2^n a$. The markets are then nested (Figure 5.1). A fourth-order supply point serving a market of radius $8a$ ships all its products (except those intended for local consumption) to the four third-order supply points located at distances $4a$. These, in turn, distribute the product to the 16 second-order centers at distances $2a;$ from these centers, the product will finally reach the first-order centers. On the other hand, the products of the third-order centers will also be supplied to the fourth-order centers — which happen to be in the market territories of all four third-order centers. Each product is thus produced in centers of one characteristic level and shipped from there to all lower- and higher-order points that lie in its market area. This division of labor is efficient as long as the local population at all centers is small compared to that of the market areas — located in a thin layer of cities serving a predominantly rural population. Otherwise, at higher-order centers with large local populations, it becomes economical to also produce lower-order products for local consumption. This in turn will increase the population of these centers and reinforce the tendency. The extreme case occurs, obviously, when a supply point also produces all lower-order goods at each level. This is sometimes called the hierarchical variant of the central place model.[2] However even making this far-reaching assumption it is clear that when higher-order points perform some of the functions of lower-order points the population will increase with level, and more complicated relationships between market size and center rank will result.

For an analysis of this situation, a link is required between the population of a center and the size of the population served by the center (or some other measure of market size). In the absence of more detailed information on the vertical division of labor and on production technology, assume that the size of any city is proportional to the population served — including that of the city itself.

In line with the principle of "nesting" developed above we also assume that, at every level, a city serves the same number — not necessarily four — of centers at the next lower level. It is now possible to calculate both city size and area population for every level of the hierarchy [A].

The result is that both city size and area population increase exponentially with a city's hierarchical level. In this

[2]Tinbergen, 1961.

respect a system of cities shows the same structure as an organization on which a constant span of control is the limiting factor at each level. The proportions in this system are determined by the size of the basic rural community, the "service ratio" of city size to population served, and the number of satellite cities per city.

Of course the structural proportions are less simple in a central-place system in which higher-order centers are not self-sufficient with respect to lower-order commodities but import certain of these from lower-order centers in their territories, a situation which we shall now examine.

FLOW MODEL

The approach outlined so far was first developed by Christaller[3] and Lösch and continued in numerous central-place studies. The most recent and expert statements have been made by Tinbergen[2] and Bos.[4]

Alternative assumptions may be made concerning the grouping of commodities that are produced in centers of a given level in this hierarchy. In fact, the optimal, that is, economically most efficient allocation of commodity production to the different levels, may be analyzed. This has been the subject of a study by Bos.[4] Its principal conclusion appears to be that no economic analysis in terms of elementary principles can be given; rather, the problem is a combinatorial one defying intuitive reasoning. But the hierarchical system compares favorably with other types of clustering in all simulation experiments.

The characteristic property of a hierarchical system of production and distribution points is that each commodity is produced in places of some level and in all places of a higher level. Thus the range of products increases as one moves up the city hierarchy. In this section an alternative view of the system of production centers is presented in

[3]Christaller, 1966.
[4]Bos, 1966.

which certain commodities flow from the agricultural base up the hierarchical ladder to centers of all orders.

We begin by relaxing the assumptions that (1) at every level cities have the same number of satellites; (2) higher-order cities contain all activities of lower-order cities plus those characteristic of their own level.

We assume as before that the economy is located in a plain of uniform fertility and we add the assumption that this plain borders on the sea on one side and that there is a single port through which all imports and exports move—an "entrepôt."

Any region so endowed will have at least two layers of settlements: rural ones, completely dispersed or clustered as villages, and the entrepôt, which functions as the economic capital of the region. The entrepôt can perform this function only when it engages in trade with the rural sector of the economy. At the most primitive stage agricultural products will be collected for export at the entrepôt and exchanged there for imported goods and urban services.

At the next stage of development, processing of agricultural commodities is introduced. This may take place in the village (or whatever the centers of lowest order are called) or at the entrepôt. In Chapter 2 it was shown that weight- and/or bulk-increasing processes occur at the point of consumption and that weight- and/or bulk-reducing activities occur at the source, unless the economies of larger scale exceed the transport cost savings so achieved.

The latter point is important: Economies of scale determine the size of the supply area from which the input material must be collected to make processing economical. This then determines the economic character of the middle towns and regulates the vertical division of labor in the system of central places. In the capital we find all those activities whose scale requirements equal or exceed the scale of the economy—and many of these activities, if not most, are at an early stage of development.

In the smallest settlements are located those activities which have constant returns to scale or require no more than the minimum scale offered by these settlements. Let us now examine some agricultural products from this point of view.

Cereals: Milling of flour reduces both bulk and weight, but flour is more apt to spoil and less easily handled in transport. Under modern technology there are considerable economies of scale. Flour milling and several processing activities for cereals are therefore found in middle towns.

Cattle: Refrigeration has made transportation of finished meat cheaper than that of cattle, but there are economies of scale in meat packing—in middle towns.

Dairy products: Processing of milk increases transportability; butter and cheese production reduce weight, and economies of scale are unimportant—in rural communities.

Canned and frozen foods: These are similar to dairy products.

Sugar: While economies of scale occur, the raw material is produced in both densely populated and densely cultivated areas. Therefore, there are also sugar refineries in both rural communities and seaports. When the raw material is imported, refining is concentrated at seaports.

Beverages: Bottling increases weight and has no important scale requirements; standard beverages are therefore produced for local use at all levels except the lowest, which cannot meet scale requirements. Production of quality beers requires special water resources; these given, it can occur in relatively small communities. Manufacturing of wines, champagne, and brandies is weight reducing but bottling is not. Buyers tend to prefer beverages bottled at the source but this is a matter of risk aversion concerning quality of product. Thus wine, brandy, and distilled beverages are produced in rural communities.

Oil milling: Oil seed, though bulkier, is more easily transported than finished oil. Oil mills enjoy economies of scale; they are located in middle towns.

Tobacco manufacturing: The early stages of processing, including drying and curing, are often performed at the source, but the making of cigars and cigarettes is subject to large economies of scale and occurs in middle towns.

Cotton: Since processing activities are more bulk reducing than weight saving, ginning is done at the source; but the later stages of processing—mainly spinning and weaving —occur under slight economies of scale in small middle towns. The last stages of processing require close contact with consumption centers since fashion and styles are all-important and subject to rapid change. Thus apparel making tends to be concentrated in or near the capital city.

Woolens and worsteds: These are similar to cotton.

Carpets and other woolen goods: These are less suscep-tible to fashion and are made in middle towns.

Lumber: Considerable reduction of weight and bulk and absence of scale economies cause the early stages to be located at the source, even outside human settlements. Later stages of finishing do not reduce weight; assembly of furniture actually increases bulk and makes this a local industry occurring at all levels of the central-place system.

Pulp and paper: Weight reducing and noxious fumes are present while economies of scale occur; since rural popula-tion densities are low in forest areas, vast territories tend to be served by the smallest rural centers so that even these can be locations of pulp and paper mills.

Hides: Hide-processing plants tend to locate next to the meat-producing industry, since the tanning of hides results in a more transportable product. Shoe production is subject to scale economies. As a fashion industry it favors locations in or near the capital city.

When agricultural raw materials are imported from abroad (additionally or exclusively), then the entrepôt will be the optimal location for all processing activities that lose weight or bulk, since this location also enjoys all advantages of scale (the only exception could be highly labor-intensive industries, as argued below). Those materials which increase bulk or weight under processing are drawn to the same loca-tion as when the agricultural raw material is grown domestically.

Are there any other activities which will have a locational advantage in small rural communities or lower-order middle towns? Now these locations may have one resource not con-sidered specifically so far: cheap labor. Thus labor-intensive industries may gravitate there, provided the product—and the inputs—are transportable enough to overcome a handicap of uneconomical distances from raw material sources and to the center of the national market. Some examples are clocks and watches, medical instruments, simple electronic devices, and parts for later assembly. Rural communities, however, rarely meet the scale requirements. A specific advantage seems to lie in handicrafts where such a tradition exists and a market organization provides the necessary contact with a national or international market.

Let us consider now those activities which process "localized" resources, that is, those found only in special locations. They are therefore produced for a larger market than the local one. Their location within the system of central places is guided by the same principles that we have developed for the processing of agricultural raw materials. (Actually, since agricultural products occur also in specialized regions, some of the following considerations apply, strictly speaking, to agricultural processing activities.) In addition to the vertical division of labor which results in a movement of products only between cities of different size-classes, there is now a horizontal one, generating as well trade between cities at the same hierarchy level. Let us consider some examples:

Iron and steel: This industry comes close to fitting the Launhardt-Weber model. Production may therefore take place neither at the raw material base (iron ore, coal) nor at the market. Technological change has drawn locations closer to the market, since economies of joint production can be achieved by integrating the further stages of processing such as casting and rolling; and these products are more costly to transport, partly because of ad valorem freight tariffs.

When iron ore is imported by sea the most favorable location is the entrepôt, since under modern technology coal weighs less than the finished product, and the above considerations for processing activities in the entrepôt apply.

Nonferrous metals: Early stages of reduction and refining save considerable weight and bulk and tend to occur at the source even if it means settling a labor force in some uninhabited region.

Oil refining and petrochemicals: These activities tend to produce a less transportable product and must be carried out large scale. They gravitate toward the entrepôt or ports.

Consider finally some activities using resources available everywhere, so-called ubiquitous resources. These are primarily the industries based on stone and clay—pottery and construction materials—and their scale requirements tend to be low. Ordinary pottery and brick yards may sometimes be found in centers of the lowest order. It is then a local activity.

Local activities include all those which result in a less transportable product and have no special scale requirement. In addition to the making of simple tools and of household goods—depending on the state of technology—such local activities include baking, cooking, and other food-finishing activities, construction, and services.

Below is a summary and classification of all economic activities in a central-place system served by a single entrepôt according to their locations. The list of items represents the division of labor among central places (when labor costs are equalized).

I. Exports to lower centers
   A. Produced in the metropolis
      1. Importation of finished goods
      2. Weight reducing processing of imported resources
      3. All activities requiring a maximum scale
   B. In middle towns, scale requirements specific to the size class of town
      1. Weight-increasing processing of materials (in particular, of ubiquitous resources)
      2. Specialized services
II. Exports to higher and lower centers; scale requirements specific to the size class of town
   A. Processing of agricultural commodities, which is weight reducing
   B. Recreational and touristic services
III. Exports to higher centers of goods produced in rural community: agricultural raw materials

IV. For local consumption; no scale requirements
  A. Processing activities which are weight increasing (in
     particular, of ubiquitous resources)
  B. Unspecialized services

When labor costs decrease with the size of town, then
some weight-increasing activities can be attracted to middle
towns which meet their scale requirements, provided they
are labor-intensive enough for labor cost savings to com-
pensate for the extra transportation cost. However, this
theoretical possibility, of which we have mentioned some examples, does not appear to be of great practical significance.

TRANSPORTATION NETWORKS

Assume that transportation takes place along a rectangular
grid of roads laid out in north-south and east-west directions.
This may be a rural road network with roads one mile apart
(the section network). Transportation costs are then determined by the sum of the horizontal (east-west) and vertical
(north-south) distances. The area which lies within a given
distance from a given point is then a square whose edges run
diagonally to the given network. It is possible to cover the
entire region without gaps or overlap with such equal-sized
squares (with due exceptions at the boundaries).

In a rural network or potential highway system we have
seen that starting from a situation where population is distributed at equal density, certain intersections will develop
into central places of various orders.

In an urban setting, if there is just one centralized activity,
it will also occupy certain corner points. These are spread
out at such distances that the market areas—the diagonal
squares surrounding them—are just sufficient for revenue to
cover costs. Of course, some activities will require the support of the entire city and some or all of the surrounding
region.

If the corner points do not offer sufficient space for central
activities, then these must be spread out along the edges,

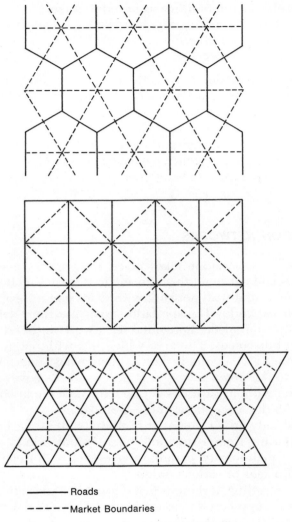

Roads
Market Boundaries

Figure 5.2. *Networks of Roads and Markets*

that is, the roads. It is not hard to see that then a hierarchy of roads will develop in the same way as the hierarchy of central places in the national economy. Thus, there will be one or a set of a few blocks which contain the most centralized activities, and each city block may be assigned a position in the hierarchy until we come to the purely residential city blocks.

But is the rectangular road grid, so often found in reality, economical with respect to transportation? There are only three possible regular networks: triangular, square, and hexagonal (Figure 5.2).

We may compare the length of roadways per unit-area under each system when the mesh width is so chosen as to equalize the average distance of points in the interior of the network.

A straightforward calculation shows that then the length of road per area is also equal. But the average distance to be covered on the network is shorter under the triangular arrangement than under the square network and even more so when compared to a hexagonal network. From a transportation point of view, triangular road systems would be the most efficient.

MATHEMATICAL NOTE

[A]

Let r be the rural population in the market area of a first order city,
p_1 the population of a first-order city,
k the factor of proportionality. Then

$$p_1 = k (p_1 + r)$$

$$p_1 = \frac{k}{1-k} r$$

where $\frac{k}{1-k}$ may be called an urban multiplier.

Now let s denote the number of satellites per city, p_n the population of an nth order center, and P_n the total population in the market area of an nth order center.

By the first assumption

$$p_n = k\, P_n \qquad (2)$$

Since, now, an nth order place also serves as center of an $n-1\ st$ order territory, the second assumption states that

$$P_n = s\, P_{n-1} + P_{n-1} - p_{n-1} + p_n \qquad (3)$$

The population served by an nth order center is composed of that of the territories served by the s satellites plus that of the own $n-1\ st$ order territory excluding the normal population of its center and substituting for it the population of the nth order center.

Substituting from (2) in (3)

$$P_n = (s+1)\, P_{n-1} - k\, P_{n-1} + k\, P_n$$

or

$$P_n = \frac{1+s-k}{1-k}\, P_{n-1}$$

$$= \left(\frac{1+s-k}{1-k}\right)^{n-1} P_1$$

Now $P_1 = r + p_1$

$$= r + \frac{k}{1-k}\, r \qquad \text{from (1)}$$

$$= \frac{r}{1-k}$$

Thus finally

$$P_n = \left(\frac{1+s-k}{1-k}\right)^n \cdot \frac{r}{1+s-k} \qquad (4)$$

and

$$p_n = \left(\frac{1+s-k}{1-k}\right)^n \frac{kr}{1+s-k} \qquad (5)$$

This shows that center size and area population are exponential functions of rank in the hierarchy. For instance if $s = 4$ and the urban multiplier is one then

k = 1/2 and the growth factor is

$$\frac{1 + 4 - 1/2}{1/2} = 9$$

From level to level, center and area populations would then increase by approximately one order of magnitude. If the largest center has a population of about 10 million, there would be room for seven levels in the hierarchy.

The hierarchical rank of a city in this analysis should not be confused with the ranking by population size which is the object of the "rank size rule." However, by introducing a random element some theoretical support may be derived for the rank-size rule from the present model.[5]

SELECTED READINGS

Beckmann, M., "City Hierarchies and the Distribution of City Size," *Economic Development and Cultural Change*, Vol. 6 (1958), pp. 243–248.

———, "Transportation Economy and Urban Concentration," in *Paths to Economic Growth*, A. Datta, ed. New Delhi: Allied Publishers, 1962, pp. 336–353.

Berry, B. J. L., and Pred, A., "Central Place Studies, a Bibliography of Theory and Applications," *Bibliography Series No. 1, Regional Science Research Institute* (1961).

Bos, H. C., *Spatial Dispersion of Economic Activity*. Rotterdam: University Press of Rotterdam, 1965.

Böventer, E. von, "Towards a United Theory of Spatial Economic Structure," *Regional Science Association Papers*, Vol. 10 (1962), pp. 163–187.

Christaller, W., *Central Places in Southern Germany*, C. W. Baskin, tr., Englewood Cliffs, N.J.: Prentice-Hall, 1966.

Lösch, A., *The Economics of Location* (translation of *Die räumliche Ordnung der Wirtschaft*, 2nd ed., 1944). New Haven: Yale University Press, 1954, Chap. 9–12.

[5]Beckmann, 1958.

Tinbergen, J., "The Spatial Dispersion of Production: A Hypothesis," *Schweizerische Zeitschrift für Volkswirtschaft und Statistik*, Vol. 97 (1961), pp. 412–419.

Ullman, E., "A Theory of Location for Cities," *American Journal of Sociology*, Vol. 46 (1940–1941), pp. 853–864.

CHAPTER **6**

Equilibrium

In the very short run all plant capacities and hence all plant locations and all household residences are fixed. What location problems remain? Essentially those of the levels of use: the extent to which the various plant capacities are utilized, the purposes to which they are put, the extent to which resource deposits are worked, and the commuting activities by which resident labor is allocated to the various plants.

Prices will perform the short-run function of rationing supplies at various locations to a spatially distributed demand. The analysis of spatial price equilibrium in the short run provides the basis for the study of equilibrium relationships in the long run.

PRICING IN SPATIALLY SEPARATED MARKETS: HOMOGENEOUS GOODS

Let demand be given in the shape of local demand functions for a single commodity depending on local price. Supply is given as follows: At each location there is a certain unit cost of production and a certain capacity (possibly nil) of producing this good. This description fits agricultural commodities where capacity reflects quality of soil and cost is the opportunity cost of local labor and other inputs; and it fits industrial production in the short run when plant capacities are fixed and supply curves horizontal.

The short-run function of the price system is to ration output and allocate supplies. The competitive price system acts so as to minimize the sum of total production and transportation cost for a given demand. As a consequence values (or rents) are also imputed to the scarce facilities — land or plant as the case may be.

We shall now examine this problem in detail for the case of industrial production. The adaptation to an agricultural situation is immediate.

Our starting point, as always in economics, is the equilibrium of supply and demand, considered now in a spatial setting. Since at market equilibrium prices are not necessarily equal, what are the equilibrium conditions, if any, that they must satisfy? In order to determine these we consider first a problem of resource allocation in a firm with branch plants which involves as a subproblem the transportation problem of linear programming.

This is the problem of how best to distribute a product from various plants to the numerous markets in which the product is demanded. In the simplest case the output of each plant is given and fixed, and so is demand at each location. Moreover, total output equals total demand. The problem is then one of minimizing transportation cost. If we consider the flows from plant to market as the unknowns, then costs — the objective function — and restrictions are all linear in terms of these flows.

While minimization of a linear function is not a classical problem of analysis, a very efficient method for calculating the solution has been developed by G. B. Dantzig: the simplex method. For our purposes the most interesting aspect is that the solution may be described exhaustively (that is, in terms of necessary and sufficient conditions) by means of a price system. This was discovered by T. C. Koopmans for an analogous problem: How shall a large shipping company or the shipping industry move empty ships from the place where they become available to the place where they are needed at minimum transportation cost?

Ships—or commodities—move efficiently when, and only when, the price system satisfies these two conditions: (1) The price difference exactly covers the transportation cost on all routes of traffic flow and (2) interlocal price differences never exceed transportation cost. The flows must, of course, satisfy the original constraints, which fix the amounts that have to be discharged at the various points [A].

The next step toward realism is to introduce costs of production at the various locations. For simplicity, assume that each plant has constant unit costs and a fixed capacity. (These will, of course, be different for different plants.) Let total demand be greater than or equal to total capacity. An example of this is the coal industry in the United States[1] and the cement industry in India.[2]

To what extent should the different plants (mines) be worked? From the point of view of economic efficiency it makes no difference whether these mines are branch plants owned by one firm or constitute a competitive industry. The problem is still one of linear programming with production costs added in the minimand and with the outflow condition relaxed so that plant capacity imposes an upper bound on outflow rather than being necessarily equal to outflow.

The resulting price system differs from the previous one in the following respects: In all plants with zero production the commodity price is less than or equal to the production cost. In all plants with positive production but some excess capacity the commodity price exactly equals production cost. When capacity is fully utilized, the commodity price exceeds production cost by a nonnegative rent. If total rent income covers fixed cost, that is, those costs arising only in the long run, then this plant should also be worked in the long run, and if rent income exceeds fixed cost the plant should be expanded.

[1]J. M. Henderson, *The Efficiency of the Coal Industry* (Cambridge, Mass.: Harvard University Press, 1958).
[2]A. Gosh, *Efficiency in Location and Interregional Flows* (Amsterdam: North Holland Publishing Company, 1965).

Notice that because of the tie-up of commodity prices with production cost the general level of prices is now no longer arbitrary but well determined. The same effect would have been achieved if commodity prices had been subjected to ceilings reflecting, say, foreign competition. These various assumptions generate special types of supply and/or demand functions: perfectly elastic up to a point and then perfectly inelastic.

The general situation in a one-commodity market is obviously the following: Given the supply and demand curves for a given commodity at a number of different locations and given the unit cost of transportation among all pairs of locations, how is the equilibrium of prices, supplies, commodity flows, and consumption determined? [B]

Interestingly enough, this problem had already been studied by A. Cournot for the case of two spatially separated markets. He noted that before and after "communication" well-defined equilibriums exist. If a commodity is transported from one location to another, in equilibrium price differences must reflect transportation costs. Thus, communication, if anything, reduces price differences. Cournot showed that interregional trade does not necessarily increase output in either quantity or value terms.[3]

What then, if anything, is increased or maximized by trade? Samuelson, writing over a hundred years later, pointed out that it is welfare as expressed by consumers' plus producers' surplus.[4] It is the maximization with respect to the commodity flows of total consumers' plus producers' surplus minus transportation costs, which may be used as a mathematical equivalent for the equilibrium conditions in a spatially extended market. Actually this "extremum principle" has been used many times before as a convenient mathematical description of competitive market equilibrium.

It should be recalled that this "surplus" is the area underneath the demand and above the supply curve. Without

[3]A. Cournot, "Of the Communication of Markets," in his *Researches into the Mathematical Principles of the Theory of Wealth* (1838), trans. by N. T. Bacon (London: Macmillan, 1897), pp. 117–127.
[4]Samuelson, 1952.

necessarily investing this concept with a welfare meaning (although this lends intuitive appeal to the approach) it is a mathematical fact that the maximization of this surplus net of transportation cost generates the conditions which determine equilibrium:

1. Net outflow of the commodity equals excess supply at this location at this price.
2. Between any pair of locations price differences do not exceed transportation cost and are equal to them when flows are positive.

Although the latter condition seems to leave a lot of leeway, in conjunction with (1) it determines prices and flows in equilibrium. The equilibrium is unique provided excess supply (supply minus demand) is everywhere an increasing function of price. These conditions remain valid if transportation is restricted to a network.

The maximum principle can be used for purposes of comparative statics. It may be shown that (1) a downward shift of an excess supply curve in one location lowers the price by the same amount in all locations that are initially in communication with this location and does not raise the price in any other location; (2) the effect of a fall in transportation cost is that prices never rise in locations (and fall in some) which are net importers and never fall in locations which are net exporters before the change.[5]

This analysis in terms of supply and demand may be carried one step farther by introducing explicitly the production activities which underlie supply curves. Natural starting points are those production activities which involve fixed input coefficients and are subject to rigid capacity limitations. This is the familiar subject of linear activity analysis.

[5]*Ibid.*

PRICING IN SPATIALLY-SEPARATED MARKETS: HETEROGENEOUS GOODS (EQUILIBRIUM IN RESIDENTIAL HOUSING)

In the face of different preferences for locations how will consumers be located so that under the existing price structure they are satisfied with locations they have attained once equilibrium is established — or is there no equilibrium?

Suppose in a given community there are a finite number of sites. As a first case consider that preferences are for sites as such regardless of where others live. Let the preference be expressed in terms of a "reservations price" for each location, that is, household. The "reservations price" is defined as the maximum price that this household is willing to pay for this site.

One can now consider the mathematical problem of finding that assignment of households to locations that is optimal in the sense of maximizing the sum of reservations prices, that is, a sum that could be extracted from all households taken together.

Since the number of households and sites is finite, there seems to be no mathematical question as to the existence of such an assignment. Does it have an economic meaning too?

To find this consider also the problem of determining equilibrium rents. The difference between reservations price and market rent measures the consumer's surplus of a site for a household. Since rents are received by site owners, maximizing the sum total of reservations prices is tantamount to maximizing consumers' and site owners' rents (surpluses). Thus maximizing the sum of reservations prices is equivalent to maximizing social welfare under the simplified assumptions of this model.

Does there always exist a system of rents which determines for each household a most preferred site and finds for each site the household which prefers it the most? For only if each household is satisfied with its site and if each site is occupied is there an equilibrium in this housing market.

The two problems turn out to be mathematically equivalent—in fact the rents are so-called "dual variables" for the linear program of assigning families to sites so as to maximize social welfare, that is, the "assignment problem."[6]

Suppose now that preferences for housing sites are influenced by housing decisions of others. In fact, let there be a given desired frequency of contacts (visits) with each of the other households; then let the most preferred site be the one for which the total time cost of making these visits is minimal. Clearly there exists (at least) one optimal assignment such that total travel time spent in making all visits is minimized. Does there also exist a set of rents or market values for sites which makes individual choices of sites conform with that optimal assignment in the sense that at those rents nobody individually would be better off under a different, that is, nonoptimal, assignment and therefore seeking to move?

Interestingly enough the answer is negative. No matter what system of rents is chosen, at least one party will prefer to move somewhere else. This is also true when preferences for sites as such are introduced additionally [C].

The mathematical proof of this paradox, "the impossibility theorem for the quadratic assignment problem," cannot be given here. It is proved in Koopmans and Beckmann.[7]

An algorithm has been proposed which uses a two-price system based on problems of this type.[8] The principal reason for the impossibility of a system of ordinary equilibrium prices is that the quadratic programming problem that is obtained from this quadratic assignment problem by relaxing the integer constraints never has integer solutions. But the conditions of market equilibrium are precisely the efficiency conditions for this quadratic programming problem.

The same assignment problem arises also when a fixed

[6]Tjalling Koopmans and Martin Beckmann, "Assignment Problems and the Location of Economic Activities," *Econometrica* (1957), pp. 53–76.
[7]*Ibid.*
[8]Alan Manne, "Plant Location under Economies of Scale—Decentralization and Computation," *Management Science*, Vol. 11, No. 2 (November, 1964), pp. 213–235.

number of plants competes for a fixed number of sites and when total transportation costs for commodity flows between plants are to be minimized.

However, when the number of locations is not fixed and distances are sufficiently small — as in a single industrial area — plants which use each others' intermediate products will tend to cluster together and to form an industrial complex, possibly even in the form of integrated plants. The "external" economies of proximity (see section below) to each other are then internalized. The converse, that industries are incompatible and suffer from each others' presence, falls under the category of negative neighborhood effects, to which we now turn.

Digression on Neighborhood Effects

The quadratic assignment problem demonstrates how an economic activity may have effects which extend to other locations and in particular spill over onto its neighborhood. The effect can be positive or negative. The negative ones include many well-known examples of "social costs": pollution of the air, causing stench and soot; and of the water, making it less fit for downstream users; noise and unsightliness.

These negative effects will be reflected in a decreased value of adjacent land. Since land values cannot become negative, this incentive may not be sufficient to attract any users at all to this land. But if users can be found, they are likely to be in the same class of noise and stench producers, for they tend to be less affected by the nuisances which they themselves create. This concentration of activities with negative spillover in the same area will be reinforced by zoning laws. (In fact, without zoning of other areas there may be no users for this land.)

Concentration of noise and smoke producers in one area does not, of course, eliminate spillover onto the neighbors of the entire area. Nor will the smoke and noise producers themselves be immune to the smoke and noise emanating from their neighbors; they will experience "external dis-economies."

Neighborhood effects can be positive. The settlement of an activity in one location may increase the attractiveness of the neighborhood for other activities. These may be similar—and competitive—or complementary. The location of a specialty store for "shopping goods" (as contrasted with so-called convenience goods) is improved when similar stores locate nearby. Their combined presence exerts a more than proportional attraction on potential customers. Thus, up to a point specialty stores tend to congregate in one neighborhood. This effect is the stronger, the greater the customers' uncertainty about the location of suppliers, the availability of the good or of substitutes, and the variety of styles—all of which make shopping around important.

Local concentration of stores, and of an industry in general, may allow the splitting off of specialized activities: transport and loading facilities, training schools, repair shops. These generate the well-known economies of scale in an industry, which are "external" to the individual firms making up the industry. Spillover effects have an important role also in residential land use. Neighborhood quarrels may arise over the seeds of weeds that are carried from one neglected backyard onto neighboring lots. Unsightliness may spill over where some houses are allowed to decay physically. The tone of the neighborhood may then be sufficiently affected to start a long decline of the area. When decisions to maintain housing are private but the effect extends to others, and this is not recoverable (not compensated for financially), there is a certain instability built in which, ultimately, accounts for the growth of slums. For suppose that some houses are allowed to deteriorate. If this is not checked, the quality of life in adjacent houses suffers. This will discourage further investment and subsequently even the level of upkeep so that the deterioration spreads. The process results in a low-level equilibrium, a slum.

Neighborhood effects finally arise in the use of congested roads, bridges, and tunnels. Each car affects the motion of nearby vehicles and delays them. Since the delay curve is rising, the average delay suffered by a car is less than the additional delay imposed by it on all traffic; consequently, social costs exceed private costs, again with far-reaching effects on the amenity of urban life. No society is really rich enough to avoid all congestion by building enough facilities. The most one can hope to achieve by an efficient use of resources is to keep congestion at the same level everywhere.[9]

EQUILIBRIUM IN A CONTINUOUSLY EXTENDED SPATIAL MARKET

If a commodity, say wheat, is produced through an extended area and is consumed everywhere, how will markets be allocated to the various supply locations?

Consider the spatial equilibrium of prices [D]. At any given point the commodity will, in general, move not in all directions but in exactly one direction: that where the increase in price just offsets transportation cost.

Locations of equal price will be arranged along continuous curves I call "isoprice" lines. The direction in which the isoprice lines approach each other most closely—also called the gradient—is that direction where the price increase per unit distance is greatest. Hence, this will be the direction of commodity flow.

It follows that commodity flow lines and isoprice lines must intersect at right angles. If transportation cost per mile is everywhere equal, then the flow lines must be straight (Figure 6.1).

If there is just one central supply region serving the entire economy, then flow lines will reach back into the interior: Their origins lie inside the supply region, and these starting points must be arranged along a curve. This curve cannot be closed unless there is inside the supply area a region of no

[9]Martin Beckmann, C. B. McGuire, and C. B. Winsten, *Studies in the Economics of Transportation* (New Haven: Yale University Press, 1956).

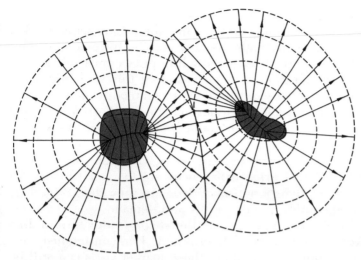

Figure 6.1. *Flow Lines and Isoprice Curves*

exports. Two "adjacent" flow lines will open up at an angle
inside of which supply and demand exactly balance. On this
curve there is a point where price is at its minimum. It may
be considered the center or most remote point of the supply
area.

From the end points of this singular curve flows move in
more than two directions. Each supply area with flows moving out in all directions must have at least one such singular
point. If it happens that the curve connecting all end points
of flow lines collapses into a point, then we have the usual
market area with a center. At this center the commodity price
is lowest. In all other respects this point is just one of many
supply points.

When several regions of excess supply exist, then there
may be several market areas. The flow lines then terminate
at a common boundary where delivered prices are equal. Inside each market area—and even inside each angle between
closely adjacent flow lines—total demand must equal total
supply. (For exports and/or imports across national boundaries an appropriate adjustment must be made.)

It may happen that in some parts of the region delivered

prices are high enough to choke off demand or that natural conditions permit no supply. Then there is no actual market in these parts, although the area may be traversed by commodity flows. Along each flow line prices must rise by the amount of transportation cost, and in this way prices are determined wherever there is a commodity flow. In the absence of such a flow, prices may be set at arbitrary levels but in such a way that the gradient never exceeds transportation cost.

There may also be certain areas which are locally self-sufficient: Local price differences are too small to pay for the costs of transportation. Prices are then determined by the local equilibrium of supply and demand.

For isolated supply points the shape of the surrounding market areas is easily determined. For continuously extended supply and demand these market areas can still be found, but only by analyzing the spatial equilibrium of prices and flows in the entire region.

This more elaborate analysis may be carried out in terms of given excess supply curves or of demand functions and production activities. Usually, when a production activity extends through an area, land is an essential input. When technology and the costs of other inputs are given, the equilibrium distribution of commodity prices will induce the spatial distribution of land rents. The spatial equilibrium of factor prices will be considered next.

FACTOR PRICING

Factor prices guide the allocation of resources. They are determined in markets where households are the suppliers and firms the demanders. For these reasons, and because factor prices are sources of income, factor pricing is usually considered separately from the pricing of commodities.

Resources may be classified according to their degree of mobility into three classes: immobile, imperfectly mobile (i.e., transportable at a cost), and perfectly mobile (i.e., transportable at zero cost). Perfectly mobile factors command the same resource price everywhere. For mobile factors interlocal price differences cannot exceed the moving cost; in fact, if equilibrium requires a steady flow of a mobile resource from one location or region to another, then the price gradient will exactly equal the moving cost. Finally, the prices of immobile resources may show any degree of regional variability and even discontinuities.

Funds are an example of perfectly mobile resources. Pure interest rates should, therefore, be equal throughout the economy. This does not rule out differences in risk premiums. To the extent that risk increases with distance, however, funds will fall into the class of (imperfectly) mobile resources.[10]

While no physical goods are perfectly mobile, lightweight intermediate or final products approach this ideal. Their geographical price differences should be negligible.

Labor is imperfectly mobile; hence, geographic wage differentials persist even in equilibrium.[11] Even when labor approaches perfect mobility, money wages will differ between locations to reflect differences in costs of living.

Let us examine how prices of consumer goods vary with the size of the community. (In addition, there may be, of course, regional differences as well.)

Von Thünen's model shows that prices of foodstuffs in the city must be higher, the larger the supply area required for the city, since transportation costs must be covered for all producers including the marginal, that is, the farthest, producer. Increasing city size raises rent at all locations closer to the city and by the opportunity cost principle puts a higher

---

[10]Lösch, 1954, pp. 461–467.
[11]*Ibid.*, pp. 455–461 and *passim.*

floor under rents in the city itself. Thus, two important items in the consumer's budget, food and housing, are increasing functions of city size.

Manufactured goods which are processed from agricultural inputs, such as textiles, furniture, and leather goods, where the optimal scale of production is small enough to allow production in small communities, will flow upward in the hierarchical system. They will be cheapest in the smallest-size community that can support their production. (For some goods, for example, special kinds of textiles, this may be only the central city.)

For all goods that are shipped down the hierarchy path, costs decrease with city size. Whether total costs of living go up with city size or fall is, therefore, a question of the composition of demand. In a poor economy living costs undoubtedly increase with community size, but in a highly industrialized country where manufactured goods make up a large portion of the demand of consumers the contrary can be the case, particularly since specialized services also tend to be available only in larger cities or even only in the leading central place.

Allocation of Immobile Resources

Local equilibrium requires that all locally available and mobile resources be allocated in a way that equalizes their marginal products. Of course, the marginal product of each factor may be different in different locations.

The movable (mobile) resources will thus seek out the opportunities offered by the immobile resources. Where mobile factors earn less than the locally going rate, that is, the local level of their marginal product, the immobile resources remain unutilized. Some immobile resources — land — have alternative uses: Their services may be consumed directly. Other immobile factors — mineral deposits — have no alternative use. The capital invested in facilities for their utilization (quarries, mines) represents sunk costs. Any return over cost is, therefore, pure rent.

This rent is the excess of intermarginal product over marginal product. A costless resource—one which has no alternative use—is utilized to the point where its marginal product is zero, that is, where payments to mobile factors exhaust marginal product. An immobile resource with alternative use in consumption, say, earns a rent only to the extent that the residual after payments to mobile factors exceeds the demand price for its direct use. All facilities earning a rent will be used for productive purposes. This rent may be due to the physical quality of the resource (a "rich" mine) or to a favorable location. If one resource at a location enjoys a location rent then all facilities of the same kind in one location will have it too.

In the short run, natural resources and sunk capital are priced in the same way. The price of sunk capital is a Marshallian "quasi-rent." In the long run the rents of capital goods will prove impermanent. Those capital goods for which rent exceeds construction costs will be expanded; those capital goods for which rent does not cover reproduction cost will be allowed to wear out. In the long run, capital goods are like "mobile resources" even though these goods may never be removed bodily.

The most important immobile factor is land and the resources it contains, including sunk capital.

Suppose that labor and land (including all capital tied up in the land) are the only resources and that labor is perfectly mobile so that its wage rates are everywhere equal (in fact they are determined by the equilibrium of total supply and demand for labor). Let commodity prices be everywhere given. Then land rent is determined as the value of output on one acre minus labor cost.

If both land and labor are immobile, local values may be imputed to land and labor separately only when there is substitutability of these two factors; the factor price ratio then equals the marginal rate of substitution. Substitutability presupposes that there is a choice of technologies for producing a single output or a choice of outputs.

Attempts have been made to separate that part of land

value which is due to physical "quality" from that which is due to "favorable location." Let us consider under what circumstances this separation is possible.

Consider an extensive region in which the land is used agriculturally. Let the physical properties of land be described in terms of the yields per acre for various products that could be produced. We assume that all inputs other than land are strictly proportional to output. These yield functions are assumed to vary continuously with location. Now in a continuously extended market, prices of various crop commodities also must vary continuously. Furthermore, input costs, essentially labor, are also continuous with respect to location. It follows that rent distribution is continuous, but the activity distribution in general is not. Rather, the von Thünen pattern is typical: discontinuous changes in land use at certain critical dividing lines, which are set up by the market. In addition, there may be natural boundaries as well: transition from plain to hills, crest lines, watersheds, rivers, etc.

Now rent due to quality is that part of rent that is in excess of what "ordinary land" at the same location or distance from markets would command. There is always a site component in rent, but for standard soil the quality component is zero.

As one moves away from the city the value of output falls and the cost of living falls, but not as rapidly (when some urban goods are consumed). If real wages are constant throughout the region, money wages are higher in relation to output prices at greater distances. And since wages equal the value of marginal product, marginal product must increase. Hence, less labor is used and the physical productivity of land declines. A fortiori the value of the marginal product of land must decline, that is, rent must fall. This conclusion is an agreement with the von Thünen model where the analysis was based on fixed proportions.

Whether the rent declines to zero depends on the accessibility of the remotest land, that is, the marginal land and the availability of labor there.

While in principle land values based on quality could vary to an extreme degree between adjacent locations, this does not happen in equilibrium. The main reason is that land values are induced by the value of services and products produced on the land, and that the latter are mobile and therefore of continuous variability. Exceptions occur only when the physical properties of land vary to an extreme degree. Thus, swamp land, although adjacent to fertile crop or grazing land, may have next to no value.

If we assume that on the outskirts of any city the rent level approximates that of the surrounding countryside — for otherwise plants would just move a short distance farther out — then that marginal land of each city is priced at about the same level everywhere. While rents will affect the location of a plant within the city — in particular its distance from the central business district — it will not exclude plants from any city. An apparent exception occurs when a fringe location is incompatible with the nature of the business, say, a specialty store. In that case this industry must compete for high-priced sites, and the rent is reflected in the product price. Thus, in no case is rent a locational factor.

OUTLOOK ON LONG-RUN EQUILIBRIUM

Long-run equilibrium requires that no activity could be profitably relocated;[12] that no piece of land (or other immobile resource) could be more profitably used; that capital is earning the same rate of return everywhere; that no mobile resource (labor) could move to a location where extra benefits (wages and nonmonetary income) exceed moving cost.

Does this imply that all resources are allocated efficiently, that is, that it is not possible to have more of some commodity at some location without having less of any other commodity at any location?

From the general theory of economic equilibrium we know that this is true provided

1. Returns to substitution are diminishing,
2. Returns to scale are constant or decreasing,

[12]*Ibid.*, pp. 94–97 and 223–262.

3. There are no indivisible factors of production,
4. There are no external economies or diseconomies.

With the exception of 1, these assumptions are all liable to be violated in a spatial economy. Therefore, one cannot assert without considerable qualification that, in general, competitive equilibrium will achieve an efficient spatial allocation of resources.

Furthermore, the equilibrium will not be unique but will depend on the path of historical development. This is most clearly seen from the indeterminacy about the precise location of the capital — the central city — and the various central places at each level of the hierarchy. Moreover, the initial condition, that is, the location of the first settlement, will affect the location of markets and the spatial pattern of prices and wages for all subsequent time, as long as relocation is costly. For then some original location will not be given up unless the economic gains at a new location are large enough to offset moving costs. Thus, moving costs constitute a frictional force which may prevent the economy from ever attaining the over-all optimal locational pattern.

Now the local or regional supply and demand functions that have been assumed must be explained by underlying data — the technology and locations of plants, and the locations of resource deposits, labor pools, and consumption centers. A complete long-run analysis would of course not stop there but would in turn explain what caused plant concentrations, and how labor sources and markets developed — would explain, in short, the distribution of human and man-made resources given the distribution of natural (but nonhuman) resources. But the powers of theory are limited. It seems more promising to attack some of the riddles of the long run through an analysis of growth processes in a spatial economy. To this we turn in the next and final chapter.

$$\sum_k x_{ik} = 1 \qquad (8)$$
$$\sum_i x_{ik} = 1 \qquad (9)$$
$$x_{ik} = 0,1 \qquad (10)$$

The total utility realized by an assignment $\|x_{ik}\|$ is $\sum_{i,k=1}^{n} a_{ik} x_{ik}$. Consider now the linear program that is obtained by relaxing condition (10)

$$\underset{x_{ik}}{\text{Max}} \sum_{ik} a_{ik} x_{ik}$$

subject to conditions (8), (9), and

$$x_{ik} \geqq 0 \qquad (11)$$

As von Neumann has shown among the solutions of the relaxed problem, the linear program, there is always one in terms of integers 0, 1, that is, there is always a solution to the original assignment problem.[13]

Now the "efficiency conditions" that characterize the solution of this linear program may be stated as follows:

Consider an optimal assignment. Let households and locations be renumbered in such a way that in this optimal assignment households are matched with locations bearing the same number. Then according to the efficiency price theorem there exists a system of consumers' surpluses, that is, values q_k for all households $k = 1, \ldots, n$ and of rents or "values" r_i for all locations $i = 1, \ldots, n$ such that

$$a_k = r_k + q_k \qquad k = 1, \ldots, n \qquad (12)$$
$$a_{ik} \leqq r_i + q_k \qquad i,k = 1, \ldots, n \qquad (13)$$

Conversely, if such a system of values exists, then it indicates an optimal assignment of households to locations.

[13]John von Neumann, "A Certain Zero-Sum Two-Person Game Equivalent to the Optimal Assignment Problem," in *Contributions to the Theory of Games*, H. W. Kuhn and A. W. Tucker, eds., (Princeton: Princeton University Press, 1953), II, 5–12.

Now condition (12) states that the utility of each residential location in an optimal assignment can be split into two parts, one a value imputed to the household, the other a value imputed to the location. Condition (13) states that the value imputed to a household is the highest consumer's surplus that this household could find in any location, where consumer's surplus is computed by subtracting the rent of the location from the utility realized in that location. Conversely, the rent imputed to a location is the highest income that it could earn by attracting any household and allowing this household to earn its highest consumer's surplus there. Assuming that such a system of rents has been established then no household would be better off in any other location and no landlord would be better off with any other than the one who resides there under the optimal assignment in question. In this sense every optimal assignment may be said to be sustained by a market mechanism in which utility maximizing tenants and income maximizing landlords respond to a system of rents.

[D]

Equilibrium in a continuous space market: Let $p(x,y)$ be the (unknown) equilibrium price at location (x,y) and let $\varphi(x,y)$ be the vector of the commodity flow. The length of the vector measures the amount of the commodity moving per unit-time in the direction of the vector. Both unknowns are to be determined jointly. The data functions are

(i) $q[x,y; p(x,y)]$ — the local excess supply of the commodity as a function of local price.

(ii) $k(x,y)$ — the unit-distance cost of transporting a commodity unit.

Suppose that the region is self-sufficient and that no exports or imports occur. At equilibrium the amount of flow generated in a location equals local excess supply

$$\operatorname{div} \varphi = q[x,y; p(x,y)] \tag{14}$$

Along any flow line price differences equal transportation cost

$$\text{grad } p = \frac{k\,\varphi}{|\varphi|} \tag{15}$$

It follows that in directions other than those of the flow lines price differences are less than transportation costs.

The (partial) differential equations (14) and (15), together with boundary conditions $\varphi_n = 0$, jointly determine p and φ.

In the special case in which excess supplies $q(x,y)$ are given independent of prices p, the equilibrium conditions are identical with the conditions for minimizing total transportation cost

$$\iint k\,(x,y) \cdot |\varphi| \, dx \, dy$$

subject to (14) as a constraint. The prices p are generated as Lagrangean multipliers; they are determined up to an additive constant while the flow field is unique.[14]

SELECTED READINGS

Beckmann, M., and Marschak, T., "An Activity Analysis Approach to Location Theory," *Kyklos*, Vol. 8 (1955), pp. 125–141. (This is an exerpt from the original reference, noted on p. vii.)

Böventer, E. von, "The Relationship Between Transportation Costs and Location Rent in Transportation Problems," *Journal of Regional Science*, Vol. 3, No. 2 (1961), pp. 27–40.

Friedmann, J. R. P., "Economy and Space," *Economic Development and Cultural Change*, Vol. 6 (1958), pp. 249–255.

Greenhut, M. R., *Microeconomics and the Space Economy; the Effectiveness of an Oligopolistic Market Economy.* Chicago: Scott, Foresman, 1963.

Hoover, E. M., *The Location of Economic Activity.* New York: McGraw-Hill, 1948, pp. 103–115.

[14]Martin Beckmann, "A Continuous Model of Transportation," *Econometrica*, Vol. 20 (1952), pp. 643–660.

Lefeber, L., *Allocation in Space. Production, Transport and Industrial Location.* Amsterdam: North Holland Publishing Company, 1958.

Lösch, A., *The Economics of Location* (translation of *Die räumliche Ordnung der Wirtschaft*, 2nd ed., 1944). New Haven: Yale University Press, 1954.

Moses, L., "A General Equilibrium Model of Production, Interregional Trade, and Location of Industry," *Review of Economics and Statistics*, Vol. 42 (1960), pp. 373–397.

Orr, E. W., "Synthesis of Theories of Location, of Transport Rates, and of Spatial Price Equilibrium," *Regional Science Association, Papers and Proceedings*, Vol. 3 (1957), pp. 61–73.

Samuelson, P. A., "Spatial Price Equilibrium and Linear Programming," *American Economic Review*, Vol. 42 (June, 1952), pp. 283–303.

CHAPTER **7**

Locational Effects of Economic Growth

Let us review the main points of this essay by considering those locational changes that are brought about by economic growth.

SPATIAL PRICE EQUILIBRIUM

Consider a single commodity and suppose that the commodity is a normal good, that is, one for which the demand increases with increasing income, other things being equal. Then, as the result of economic growth the demand curve will shift to the right in at least one location while no shift to the left occurs at any location. A right shift of demand will increase price in that location and—by the same amount —also in all other locations which are connected to this location through commodity flows in either direction on the assumption that supply has not increased, or has increased less than demand has. Prices are unchanged at other locations. Of course, the more locations a point is connected to, the more elastic is excess supply; therefore, the smaller the local impact—but the more widespread the regional impact—of a local growth in demand. Demand shifts in the same direction at several locations will reinforce each other. It is conceivable that a commodity may be a normal good in one location and an inferior good in others due to differences in local possibilities of substitution (for example, beer may be inferior in a wine-growing region but superior in cities). Then the net effect on the price of the commodity at its source determines the price level elsewhere.

GROWTH OF FIRMS

Consider an isolated supplier. As incomes rise and demand shifts to the right, the boundary line of zero demand will move outward in strict proportion to the shift in the intercept of the demand curve, as long as price at the supply point remains unchanged.

In the case of a supply area serving a given market point, price will rise by the extra transportation cost to the marginal supply location. An increase in demand by constant amounts will lead to smaller and smaller increases in the distance, since distance to the farthest supplier increases with the square root of total demand. If the price rise at the demand point and at all other locations increases supply at all locations, then the supply area will increase by even less.

In the special case of water the supply area will increase discontinuously as new watersheds are being tapped. However, this requires penetrating the barriers that separate the newly added from the already utilized watersheds.

Consider next the effect of a rising demand on the price policy of firms. An isolated supplier (a spatial monopolist) responds to a parallel shift to the right of the local demand curve by raising his price—and the quantity sold. Although total demand at the mill gate is not a linear function of price if linear local demand curves are assumed, the conclusion applies also to sales in a region. We recall that the optimal mill price is three-fourths of marginal cost plus one-fourth of the maximum price. To an upward shift of the local demand curves by one price unit, the isolated supplier as a monopolist responds by raising his price by one-fourth of a unit. Since this is less than the demand shift, his market area is now even larger than before the demand shift. Similarly under uniform pricing the profit-maximizing price increase is three-fourths the upward shift of the demand curve (the optimal price being one-fourth of the marginal cost plus three-fourths of the maximum price), and the area of delivery is farther extended.

The perfectly discriminatory price at the mill is one-half of the marginal cost plus one-half the maximal price and rises by half the rate of transportation cost. The price level is therefore raised by half the amount of the demand shift, and again the market area is extended.

In the same way it can be seen that cost increases raise prices but not by the full amount. The net effect is then always a decrease of the market area; the converse happens with a cost decrease.

The over-all conclusion is that upward shifts of demand induce price increases but of such magnitude that sales are also increased. Market areas are extended where possible. Since potential sales areas then overlap to a greater extent, competition or rather rivalry is intensified. Profits per area are also increased so that the stakes become bigger.

Historically, economic growth has tended to lower transportation cost relative to prices of other goods and services partly because of economies of scale, but mainly because of technical change. The effect of this is to extend the market areas of low-cost suppliers at the expense of those of high-cost suppliers and to reduce interlocal price differences.

What is the effect on the price level, on consumption, and on the total demand for transportation?

Consider first an isolated supplier. It can be seen that the monopoly price is an increasing function of unit transportation cost.[1] Under perfect discrimination the market radius is extended, and the price distance function is shifted

[1]See mathematical notes [C]–[E] of Chapter 3 for the derivation of the monopoly prices.

downward for all points. While the mill price is unchanged, total prices are lower. A uniform delivered price is not affected by changes in transportation cost, but the area of delivery is increased.

When market areas are contiguous or overlap the conclusions remain valid with only minor modification. Even when the neighboring firms do not change prices after an upward shift of demand, it would pay a firm (that is, increase its profit), to raise its own price as long as the other prices remain unchanged, and its profits would rise even more when the other firms follow suit. The same is true when marginal costs increase. When costs decrease a firm should want to lower prices even when others are expected to maintain theirs. The only deterrent would be the risk of starting a round of mutual undercutting—a price war—which is particularly risky under uniform pricing.

The over-all conclusion is then that downward shifts of transportation costs, while not changing mill prices, uniform delivered prices, or the discriminatory price at the mill gate, will tend to increase the actual or potential sales area, the quantities sold, and the profits made. And this is true also when prices are fixed and/or sales territories are allocated by agreement. When transportation costs fall to zero, the entire economy becomes the market area under contention.

Finally we may consider the demand for transportation itself. The demand for transportation tends to be elastic with respect to transportation cost. This was demonstrated by the early railway economist, D. Lardner. For the special case of a supplier serving an unrestricted circular market area where demand is subject to the same demand curve everywhere, calculation shows elasticity of the demand for transportation to be 2. For situations with competing suppliers this value is an upper bound.[2]

The downward movement of transportation rates is slowed or even arrested when congestion effects and other diseconomies of scale make supply of transportation a sharply

[2]Martin Beckmann, "Bemerkungen zum Verkehrsgesetz von Lardner," *Weltwirtschaftliches Archiv*, Vol. 69, No. 2 (1952) pp. 199–213.

increasing function of traffic volume. (In the long run, congestion may be avoided, but only at increasing cost by supplying additional facilities.)

When demand increases as a result of economic growth, plants that have been operating below capacity will be induced to increase output, and shut-down plants may be put back into operation. If production is governed by fixed technological coefficients, then, as in all linear programming situations, the response will be discontinuous: There are critical prices at which a discontinuous shift in output will be made. Unless price rises from its current level to above the next critical threshold level no response by the firm will be forthcoming.

Once all capacities are fully utilized the system cannot increase output in the short run, and increased demand merely leads to increased price unless it is filled by imports. If the commodity is inferior or superseded by a new substitute, one plant after another may reduce its output until all plants are shut down; the plant at the most favorable location — in terms of the highest local demand prices and/or smallest unit costs — will be the last to cease production.

INDUSTRIAL DYNAMICS

In a growing economy new openings will appear for plants. The gaps between plant sites will be closed in the order of their size. When the initial distribution was irregular, such irregularities will persist though on a smaller scale.

Even in a growing economy, not all industries will grow. If an industry is declining or mistakes have been made in plant location, some plants will go bankrupt. The emerging pattern indicates the survival of the feasible and the extinction of the unfeasible locations.

Assume now a homogeneous region with uniform demand density and a hexagonal roster of supply points for a given product. As demand grows profits of producers rise from their initial level of zero and finally reach a level where new plants can enter the market profitably. The best location for a new plant would seem to be not at the site of the existing plants but as far removed from them as possible. These locations will be at the centers of those equilateral triangles that can be spanned by any three neighboring suppliers. Since each of the existing points is involved in six such triangles, the number of supply points will be tripled as these central locations become occupied.

Suppose, however, that demand has doubled. Then new plants could locate and still break even provided they placed themselves right next to the existing plants. Only when demand is more than tripled are new locations more profitable for a new plant. This is another manifestation of the Hotelling paradox already discussed in a static context (see the section on duopoly in Chapter 3) which generates a socially costly concentration of like producers in the same location. The case for locating at existing plant locations is strengthened if population density and hence local demand are higher at established locations. In a city hierarchy plants will be duplicated—or in the case of constant-cost firms, be expanded—in central places of one level before taking the jump to lower-order centers.

This jump will definitely be made when demand has tripled, for at the new in-between locations profits are higher once demand approaches the triple level. In fact since the extra plants at existing locations must now be forced out losses will be made at the old locations. Development of an industry may thus take place in a leapfrog manner.

This jump is made easier in a city system which is not spaced at exactly equal distances and has different populations in cities of equal rank. As gaps between supply points are being filled out, economic growth results in a more homogeneous distribution of suppliers. Except for the supply of localized resources production will to an increasing extent be to fill local demand and for a smaller and smaller tributary area. In this sense production and consumption locations tend to move closer together as an economy grows.

STRUCTURAL CHANGES IN AGRICULTURE

A growth model of agricultural supply areas combines the changes of its various supply zones. As each of these grows larger, the limit of cultivation is pushed outward and marginal transportation costs and rents rise.

In the absence of technical change the central city cannot grow indefinitely. Even before its entire population is engaged in transportation activities it must reach a limit where just enough labor remains to produce the industrial commodities needed to meet the increased demand by the receivers of rent in the rural areas. In fact, from initial equilibrium the city can grow only by reducing per capita income of city dwellers or through capital accumulation which increases the city laborer's productivity. As the maximal size of the city is reached, a new entrepôt must be founded to become the nucleus of another "isolated state" located in a fertile wilderness.

The maximal size of a city is dependent on the following facts. Urban workers exchange their product with marginal land cultivators on such terms that their food intake is at the subsistence level. Of course, agricultural production may take place outside the market area of the city, that is, beyond the maximal distance within which it pays to ship agricultural products. These farms will have to be self-sufficient. If land is abundant, self-sufficiency is possible at a level above the barest minimum necessary for survival. This level of living will set the "subsistence" standard that prevails at the border of the market economy. If urban labor is mobile and is willing to settle in these remote hinterlands, then the same level of subsistence will be approached in the city as the city reaches its maximum size.

If land is limited and an increasing population presses against this limit, then a Malthusian equilibrium will result, with a standard of living just sufficient to keep the average size of population constant. In an otherwise peaceful economy this means that average mortality just balances average nativity per capita. Hunger and disease will be the regulators. This has marked the end of growth in certain underdeveloped regions.

As the zone of cultivation spreads it can support another city. Several "isolated states" may then exist side by side with little or no trade. If the state of technology in inter-urban transportation permits, cities will engage in exchange. This will be particularly advantageous as long as the cities are of different sizes.

DYNAMICS OF CENTRAL PLACES

Increasing efficiency of agriculture reduces the number of persons to be employed per acre of agricultural land. As a result, the countryside is increasingly depopulated. The central places of lowest order will then require fewer people to serve the area; and as the attraction of the more populous higher-order centers increases and the relative cost of trans-portation decreases, the lowest-order centers will be eroded and may even disappear. Technical change may have a dif-ferent impact on different levels of the city hierarchy and may thus change their relative sizes.

Consider now the effect of economic growth on city size in the absence of technical change. In an underdeveloped economy with low per capita incomes most consumption will be of agricultural goods while per capita demand for industrial products will be low, even though total demand may still be large, owing to the size of total population. Under extreme poverty, however, industrial production — the modern sector of the dual economy — will be concentrated in the economic capital of the nation no matter how large the country. By contrast handicraft production in small-scale establishments will be as dispersed as population, and thus located in the central places of the lowest order. There is thus no locational advantage in intermediate cities. These tend to be absent or rare, and where they occur their function is primarily political, military, and administrative. All industries will start out with one plant, and its optimal location will be invariably at or near the economic capital. As demand grows for the product of industries in which initially one plant was sufficient to meet the national demand, it becomes possible for more plants to enter. While these will at first locate in the central city due to the Hotelling phenomenon, from a certain point on they will be located in central places of the next order. The effect then is a decentralization of production, increased competition, and the growth of intermediate cities: regional capitals. This process may be described as "allometric growth" a term borrowed from biology. This means that the relative size of a city grows along with the total size of the economy but at a rate which in general is different from the over-all (absolute) rate of growth.[3]

ECONOMIC GROWTH IN A ONE-PRODUCT ECONOMY

Consider an economy which uses just one commodity that can be produced everywhere and can serve as consumption and capital good. In the simplest case — corresponding to the macroeconomic growth models of general economic theory — production conditions are homogeneous everywhere. Initially let population be distributed at a uniform density throughout a strip area bordering on one edge of a rectangularly shaped economic region — the "eastern seaboard" of a large continental state. We now consider the following growth model: (1) Population grows by reproduction and/or immigration at a constant rate, (2) a constant proportion of income is saved, (3) a single commodity is produced which also serves as capital good, and (4) the production function which determines output as a function of labor, capital, and land is homogeneous of degree one and has the usual properties of positive marginal products and diminishing returns to substitution.

Since land is free, it will be used to the point where its

[3]Martin Beckmann, "City Hierarchies and the Distribution of City Size," *Economic Development and Cultural Change*, Vol. 6 (April, 1958), pp. 243–248.

marginal product is zero. We may disregard it as far as the proportions in which capital and labor are used are concerned. From neoclassical growth theory we know that a process of balanced growth is generated where capital and labor — and now also land in use — maintain the same proportions and hence grow at the same rate.

This will cause the "frontier" of land cultivation to move west at a speed which is proportionate to the area already occupied. This phase of the growth process is ended when the entire rectangle is occupied. From then on labor and capital alone will grow, and returns to scale will diminish. But the density of activities will be the same everywhere. So much for growth in a perfectly homogeneous economic environment.

Consider now an economy no longer regionally homogeneous but still producing and consuming just one product. At each location population and demand grow at a certain local rate not necessarily uniform and not necessarily positive everywhere. Suppose that a constant amount of total output is saved and that this is invested at the various locations so as to equalize the rate of return to capital. If the commodity — and that includes capital — and the population are perfectly mobile, only the national growth rates of population and capital stock are relevant. The mobile resources — labor and capital — will be allocated first to those pieces of land having the highest yield. From these patches cultivation will spread outward, provided yield is a continuous function of location. In addition, there will spring up new centers of cultivation as the nationally uniform rate of return falls to the level achievable in such places. At the same time, under a regime of neoclassical production functions, the area already cultivated will be used more intensively. However, this entire expansive process is subject to diminishing rather than constant returns to scale, since local returns are diminishing owing to the limitation of land.

What would an economic system look like in which land acted merely as a "catalyst," determining the local rates of yield on inputs of capital and labor but not imposing any limitation of its own? Under those circumstances, as long as capital and labor grow at the same rate locally, so would product. Is an economy with locally different rates of human fertility (or net reproduction of population) and of saving capable of a growth equilibrium?

A spatial equilibrium with prices that are constant over time but locally different must exist such that the rate of growth of capital and labor is the same at all locations and such that the necessary migration of labor and flow of commodity for both accumulation and consumption is maintained. (We assume unit transportation cost to be independent of the volume of flow.) The question is whether this equilibrium is attained from every initial position and will be maintained under a growth process. This can be settled only by considering a mathematical model of this space market, allowing for disequilibrium and for adjustment processes. The answer will obviously depend on the nature of this adjustment process. It is plausible that such an equilibrium, if possible, will also be attained from every initial position under the usual conditions for stability of competitive equilibrium—but that cannot be demonstrated here.

In one possible equilibrium pattern under the assumptions made here, extreme regional concentration of growth occurs in a few centers—"singular points" of the flow fields. Such a growth process would have far-reaching consequences for the locational structure of an economy. Perhaps it is only the dispersion of localized resources that counterbalances such forces of concentration.

For an equilibrium growth process, the locations where the net rate of reproduction of the population is below zero must make up the deficit by a continuous stream of immigrants from regions where the rate of reproduction is above the national average. Deficiencies in capital accumulation similarly must be made up by a stream of the capital good from regions where the savings rate exceeds the national average. To induce such streams of population and of the commodity, interregional differences in the real wage rate and in the price of the capital good must prevail. A mathematical analysis shows that under stationary conditions an equilibrium of prices and commodity flows exists;[4] and an equilibrium of that labor flow (migration) which preserves the spatial distribution of population and of economic activities also exists.

Formally it is only a small step to an analysis of equilibrium for a growing economy. As long as scale effects are absent in both production and transportation, an equilibrium which is possible at some level will be possible at all levels. We may conclude that a spatial equilibrium with prices that are constant over time but locally different exists such that the rate of growth of capital and of labor is the same at all locations and such that the necessary migration of labor and flow of commodities for both accumulation and consumption are maintained.

LOCALIZED RESOURCES

These cannot be decentralized, but as less favorable resource deposits are worked, the supply tends to come from more widely dispersed supply points. Technical change will tend to increase the degree of fabrication and will tend to reduce the weight of inputs while, possibly, constantly increasing the weight and bulk of commodities. This tends to reduce the transportation costs of inputs in relation to per-unit-output costs and, therefore, tends to reduce the attractive force of resource deposits in the Weberian triangle. As a result, the location of a production activity processing localized resources will be governed more by the hierarchy of central places and be pulled away from original resource locations. This does not apply to the initial stages of reducing and refining the material.

As more localized resources are discovered, population will be dispersed or concentrated depending on whether additional resource locations tend to be close to or farther removed from existing deposits. Clearly, both types of dis-

[4]Martin Beckmann, "A Continuous Model of Transportation," *Econometrica*, Vol. 20 (1952), pp. 643–660.

covery occur, with the latter type more likely in the long run.

Perhaps not the least important aspect of economic growth is that it tends to generate more homogeneity by permitting deconcentration in the spatial structure of an economy, a wider diffusion of products, and a tendency toward equilibrium of price structures.

In conclusion it may be fairly said that we are just beginning to understand the economic impact of growth on location. For that matter, as the attentive reader will have noticed, unsolved and imperfectly understood problems abound throughout location theory.

SELECTED READINGS

Berman, E., "Spatial and Dynamic Growth Model," *Regional Science Association, Papers and Proceedings*, Vol. 5 (1959), pp. 143–150.

Borts, G. H., and Stein, J. L., *Economic Growth in a Free Market.* New York: Columbia University Press, 1964.

Friedmann, J. R. P., "Locational Aspects of Economic Development," *Land Economics*, Vol. 32 (1956), pp. 213–227.

Hodge, G., "The Prediction of Trade Center Viability in the Great Plains," *Papers of the Regional Science Association*, Vol. 15 (1965), pp. 87–115.

Hoover, E. M., *The Location of Economic Activity.* New York: McGraw-Hill, 1948, pp. 145–212.

Melamid, A., "Some Applications of Thünen's Model in Regional Analysis of Economic Growth," *Regional Science Association, Papers and Proceedings*, Vol. 1 (1955), pp. 51–55.

North, D. C., "Location Theory and Regional Economic Growth," *Journal of Political Economy*, Vol. 63 (1955), pp. 243–258.

Rapkin, C., "Some Effects of Economic Growth on the Character of Cities," *American Economic Review, Papers and Proceedings of the American Economic Association*, Vol. 46 (May, 1956), pp. 293–301.

Authors' Index

Ackley, G., 58
Alonso, W., 64n, 71n
Arnold, E., 7n

Balinski, M. L., 20n
Baumol, W. J., 20n
Beckmann, M., vii, 19, 86n, 95, 95n, 98n, 111n, 116n, 121n
Berman, E., 125n
Berry, B. J. L., 87n
Bertrand, J., 36
Borts, G. H., 125n
Bos, H. C., 48, 77, 87n
Böventer, E. von, 73n, 87n, 11n
Bunge, W., 7n

Chisholm, M., 71n
Christaller, W., 77, 87n
Clark, J. M., 58n
Cooper, L., 20n
Cournot, A., 35, 35n, 36, 92, 92n

Dantzig, G. B., 62n, 90
Dennison, S. R., 18n
Dewey, D., ii, 36n, 42n
Dunn, E. S., Jr., 71n

Edgeworth, F. Y., 36
Efroymson, M. A., 21n
Egbert, A., 71n

Feldmann, E., 21n
Fetter, F., 38n, 58n
Friedmann, J. R. P., 111n, 125n

Garrison, W. L., 19n
Grosh, A., 91n
Greenhut, M., 7n, 24n, 38n, 58n, 111n
Gülicher, H., 21n

Hagget, P., 7n
Hamburger, M. J., 21n
Heady, E., 71n
Henderson, J. M., 71n, 91n
Hodge, G., 125n
Hoover, E. M., 7n, 24n, 58n, 71n, 111n, 125n
Hotelling, H., 40, 58n, 118, 121
Hyson, C. D., 58n
Hyson, W. P., 58n

Isard, W., 6n, 7n, 37n

Koopmans, T. C., vii, 90, 95, 95n
Kuehn, A. A., 21n
Kuenne, R. E., 16n
Kuhn, H. W., 16n, 109n

Lardner, D., 116
Launhardt, W., 15, 20, 28, 28n, 81
Lav, M. R., 43n, 48n, 58n
Lefeber, L., 102n
Lehrer, F. A., 21n
Lösch, A., 7n, 9n, 24n, 29n, 43, 44, 58n, 71n, 77, 88n, 101n, 112n

Machlup, F., 58n
Malthus, T. R., 119
Manne, A. S., 24n, 95n
Marble, D. F., 19n
Marschak, T., vii, 111n
Marshall, A., 103
McGuire, C. B., 98n
Melamid, A., 125n
Meyer, W., 24n
Miksch, L., v, 26, 26n
Mills, E. S., 43n, 48n, 58n
Morgenstern, O., 37n
Moses, L., 23, 41, 59n, 112n

Neumann, J. von, 37n, 109n
North, D. C., 125n

Organization for European Cooperation and Development, 71n
Orr, E. W., 112n

Palander, T., 7n, 65n
Pfouts, R. W., 38n, 58n
Pick, G., 16
Ponsard, C., 7n
Pred, A., 87n

Rapkin, C., 125n
Ray, T. L., 21n
Reilly, W. J., 30n, 50

Samuelson, P. A., 92, 92n, 112n
Singer, H. W. A., 31n
Smithies, A., 58n
Stein, J. L., 125n
Stigler, G. J., 58n
Stocking, G. W., 38n, 58n
Stouffer, W. A., 30n

Thünen, J. H. von, 26, 29, 60–64,
70, 101
Tinbergen, J., 76n, 77, 88n
Tucker, A. W., 109n

Ullman, E., 88n

Varignon, P., 18

Warntz, W., 39n
Watkins, M. W., 38n, 58n
Weber, A., 7n, 15, 18n, 20, 24n, 81
Wingo, L., 64n, 71n
Winston, C. B., 98n
Wolfe, P., 20n

Zipf, G. K., 39n

Subject Index

Region, 13, 27, 67, 99
Regional science, 6
Relocation, 39–41
Rent, 13, 49, 62, 91, 94, 101, 102–105
Reproduction, 121
Resources, 9, 10, 14, 63, 103
    deposits, *See* Deposits
    local, 14, 81, 118, 124
    special, 11, 12, 68
    ubiquitous, 82
Retail Gravitation, Law of, 30, 50
Returns to scale
    constant, 5, 67, 105, 122
    decreasing, 122
    increasing, 5, 32
    See also Economies of scale
Rhode Island, 12
Roads, 65, 73, 83–85
Rotation, 62

Sales, 9, 27, 28, 29, 115
Satellite city, 29, 67, 77
Search process, 21
Service ratio, 77
Services, 68, 82, 102
Shopping trips, 11, 39
Short-run
    analysis, 6
    period, 26
    problems, 25
Simplex method, 90
Slum, 97
Smoke, 96
Space, 3, 4, 35, 66, 83
Specialization, agricultural, 63
Spillover, 96, 97
State
    isolated, 63, 119, 120
    stationary, 123
Statistics, comparative, 93
Stone, and clay, 82
Strong model, 18
Substitutes, 11, 103

Sugar, 14, 79
Supply, 12, 22, 92
    area, 14, 15
    See also Market area

Tanning, 14
Technology, 8, 62, 63, 100, 106
    change, 81, 119, 120, 124
Textiles, 12, 102
von Thünen, rings, 61–63
Tobacco, 79
Tourism, 82
Toys, 12
Traffic, 18, 98
Transportation, 10, 16, 20, 68, 73
    See also Costs, Transportation
Travel time, 64, 98
Truck gardening, 62

Uncertainty, 25, 101
Unemployed, 12
U.S. Steel Corporation, 15
Utility, 9, 10

Valley, 12, 22
Vertex, 18, 22, 40

Wage differentials, 19, 101
Warehouse, 20n, 21
Waterways, 60, 65
Weberian triangle, 16–17
Weight, 14, 15, 16, 22, 68, 124
Welfare, 9, 92, 94
    economics, 4, 96–98
Wool, 14, 80

Zoning, 96